Contents

CW00601666

Introduction

Crystals have been used as healing tools for millennia. It is only recently that they have become accessible to the layperson through the vast amount of literature (and courses) available on the subject.

It is important to realise that although certain crystals are aligned to healing particular areas of the mind, body and spirit, a lot of the knowledge is based on the individual's or healer's intuition.

In this booklet I will briefly discuss the history of crystal healing and how it works, including examining the energy system that crystal healing is based upon.

I will explain the properties of several crystals and show you a few of the ways in which you can use them to influence and improve your well-being.

An essential aspect of crystals is their care and maintenance. This is often forgotten by lay practitioners and so may be causing 'bad' energetic influences. To this end I have included a section on cleansing and purifying crystals.

Crystal healing is a wonderfully simple art and I hope that after reading this book you will go on to include these marvellous artefacts in your life.

The past

Crystals have been used as healing tools for thousands of years. In this section I will take a brief trip through time to visit some of these uses.

Aztecs, Incas and Mayans are just some of the civilisations that arose and fell in Central and South America. The peoples of these civilisations were attuned to the land and spirits in ways that have been lost to us. Fragments of history gathered by archaeologists and anthropologists suggest that these wise people used crystals in their arcane arts.

Native American methods of healing were as wide and diverse as any that have come since. Within the lore passed down through word of mouth comes the healing knowledge of crystals.

Cherokee tribes used crystals to diagnose illnesses as well as for divination. They believed that crystals were living entities and 'fed' them on the blood of deer.

The people of the Nile have, for thousands of years, been aware of the healing properties of gems. Perhaps the oldest preserved medical document, the *Egyptian Ebers' Papyrus,* has been dated to around 1500BC.

The papyrus mentions several crystal therapies; in particular, it records the properties of such beautiful gems as the lapis lazuli. This gem, it says, aids the healing of eye infections and cataracts.

The tomb of Tutankhamum was made out of quartzite and contained 143 jewelled amulets; each believed to have magical powers.

In Rome around AD 70, Gaius Plinius Secundus (known as Pliny the Elder) recorded a massive repertoire on the natural world (*'The Nature of Things'*). This 37-volume work mentioned healing crystals several times.

In the Bible, crystals are mentioned. Twelve stones were chosen to represent the twelve tribes of Israel. These stones were placed upon the High Priest Aaron's breastplate.

These were sardius, topaz, carbuncle, emerald, sapphire, diamond, ligure, agate, amethyst, beryl, onyx and jasper. The breastplate provided 'magical' protection for Aaron.

Vikings, those pirate traders of a thousand years ago, used crystals in their healing rituals, particularly favouring amber as a luck bringer.

The agate crystal was used by Vikings to divine the location of hidden or lost treasure.

Jade is one of the most prized stones of the Maoris of New Zealand. They believe that these stones, particularly ones that are a dark olive-green, are bringers of good fortune.

According to a Chinese encyclopaedia dated around 1596, a drink made of jade, rice and dew water would harden the bones, calm the mind and strengthen the muscles.

We have seen that peoples across time and space have used crystals in their healing practices. In the next section I will speculate on how crystal healing works.

How crystal healing works

There is an energy that pervades all of creation. This energy flows and ebbs throughout the universe, through the stars and planets and through you and me.

People around the world have alluded to this energy in several ways but the way they describe it leaves no doubt that they are speaking of one and the same thing.

To explain how crystal healing works requires an understanding of this energy system and our interactions with it.

Chi

The Chinese call it 'chi', Indians call it 'prana' and the Japanese refer to it as 'ki'. Within this book I will refer to it as chi.

Let us stop and consider the implication and wonder of this unimaginable energy.

- ❑ There are people who have had mystical experiences, during which they felt a connection with the universe. It is not inconceivable to suggest that they have sensed this living energy, chi.
- ❑ Masters of martial arts perform feats that are incredible. They do this through the direct manipulation of chi.
- ❑ Geomancers, those who have an understanding of the flow of energy within the environment, practice their art (feng shui) to bring people and their living and working areas into harmony.

Delving further into the knowledge passed down from master to disciple we understand that as this energy passes through the body it encounters whirls or eddies.

Each of these whirls or vortices is more commonly known as a chakra point (indeed chakra translates as "spinning wheel" or "vortices").

These chakras and the energy that flows through them are intimately related to our wellbeing, whether it is physical, emotional, mental, or spiritual.

Aura

Another energetic phenomenon that exists around our body is the human aura. This field is three-dimensional in that it is egg-shaped with the body in the centre.

From across the globe, many people describe this field in similar ways and some with the odd small discrepancy, but on the whole they agree on the following aspects.

- There are (at least) seven distinctive layers to the aura, each having different characteristics.

- The aura is associated with the chakra energy system. Indeed, it is speculated that the interaction of the chakras with the human body creates the aura energy.

- The aura provides energy links to other creatures, people and the universe.

- Auras can be of different sizes and different shades of colour.

You should not read, or try to read, a person's aura without their permission. Consider for a moment - this is tantamount to giving them an intimate health check, which you would not do without their consent.

There is a complex, symbiotic and dynamic interchange of energy between the aura, body, chakras and chi. So much so that it takes a lifetime of experience to bring any kind of understanding to it.

Here are just a few words to give you a flavour of the aura layers:

The etheric layer:

- Is connected with the root chakra
- Is intimately associated with the physical body
- Is said to impart instructions at a genetic level to cells to become the different functioning parts of the body.

The emotional layer:

- Is associated with the sacral chakra
- Is linked to our emotions and as such is 'seen' as an ever- flowing mix of energy
- People who are sensitive to seeing energy tap into this layer most often.

The mental layer:

- Is reflected in the solar plexus chakra
- Is associated with thoughts and mental processes
- Interpretation of information according to belief structures is done within this layer.

The astral layer:

- Is associated with the heart chakra
- Contains the essence of our personality
- Is concerned with relationships particularly in the sense of encompassing humanity.

The causal layer:

- Is associated with the throat chakra
- Is linked to the collective unconscious
- Is the doorway to higher levels of consciousness.

The celestial layer:

- Is linked to the third eye chakra
- Is the layer where psychic creativity, e.g., spell casting exists
- Is the least likely layer to be seen by sensitive people.

The ketheric layer

- Is associated with the crown chakra
- Is a container and integrator for all the other layers
- Has access to all universal energies
- Maintains the individuality of each being.

Chakras

To reiterate, chakras are whirling vortices of energy that are contained within the auric field (and body) of living creatures.

These spinning vortices of energy are part of the subtle energy system that forms the basis of an ancient Eastern approach to healing our physical, mental and spiritual selves.

Although the seven main chakras are described here, ancient texts refer to as many as 88,000 chakras upon and within the human form.

As we shall see each chakra is associated with various physical, psychological and spiritual characteristics.

A blockage in the energy flow through any of the chakras can manifest itself as a problem with its related features.

Headaches could be caused by an imbalance of energy in the brow or the crown chakra.

In this section I will examine each chakra and its related features, beginning with the root chakra.

Root or base chakra

The muladhara (meaning 'root' or 'support') chakra is located at the base of the spine and is associated with the colour red.

The root chakra controls the flow of energy into the body. Working at its optimum, this chakra can help in resolving problems experienced with the kidneys, adrenal glands, spinal column, and colon. It can also strengthen our survival and self-preservation instincts.

Sacral chakra

The svadhisthana (which means sweetness) chakra is located in the lower abdomen and is associated with the colour orange.

A misaligned sacral chakra can cause problems with the sexual organs, spleen, genitals, and bladder. It is also linked with our emotions and needs.

Solar plexus chakra

The manipura (meaning 'lustrous green') chakra can be found just above the navel. It is associated with the colour yellow.

This chakra is your personal power centre. Developing the solar plexus chakra can help increase willpower and build motivation.

Bodily areas that are related to this chakra are digestion, metabolism, and the nervous system. Also associated with it are the pancreas, gall bladder, nervous system, liver, stomach, and adrenal glands.

Heart chakra

The anahata (meaning 'sound that is made without any two things striking') chakra is located in the centre of the chest. Its colour associations are green and pink.

This chakra governs emotions to do with the heart. It is known to affect the intuitive ability of clairsentience.

Improving the heart chakra can help balance the emotions of giving, receiving, losing, and acquiring love.

In physical terms, it will aid organs such as the heart, lungs, thoracic areas and circulation.

Throat chakra

The vishuddha (meaning 'purification') chakra is situated close to the Adam's apple at the centre of the neck. It is associated with the colour blue.

The throat chakra governs communication and deals with issues of expressing speech, thoughts, and writing.

For those who have difficulty expressing their emotions, try working on the throat and the heart chakra. *Fiona, Denmark*

Working with the throat chakra is known to improve the intuitive ability of clairaudience.

Energising the throat chakra can aid the glands of the throat and is known to have a healing effect on the mouth, ears and upper respiratory system.

Brow or third eye chakra

The ajna (meaning 'to perceive' or 'to know') chakra is located at the front of the head on the forehead between the eyebrows and just above the bridge of the nose. The colour associated with this chakra is indigo.

As your psychic centre, the brow chakra has been depicted in many cultures as the 'third eye'. Working with this chakra aids seeing in all aspects of life.

Energising the brow chakra can affect dreams, imagination, concentration, intuition, wisdom and the intuitive ability of clairvoyance. Physically it aids the upper glands in the facial region, eyes, nose and ears.

Crown chakra

The sassasrara (meaning 'thousandfold') chakra is located at the top of the head and from this point extends above the head about an inch. The associated colours of this chakra are gold, violet and white.

This is your spiritual centre. Energising the crown chakra can assist us in creating our link to spirit guides, angelic sources and our higher self.

The crown chakra can work with all issues that affect us on a spiritual level. It also helps in blending spirituality with our earthly personalities.

A fully energised crown chakra can help conditions to do with the head and brain.

Tuning the orchestra

As we have seen, chi flows through the universe in a constant, unending stream.

It touches all - matter, energy and spirit alike. It is the universal connector. All things are influenced by its passage.

Just as a maestro conducts music without physically playing any instrument, chi flows through the universe conducting its affairs.

If the flow of chi is stagnant, resisted and blocked then we must expect illnesses, disease, and discord.

Should one of the chakras be out of alignment, the whole section that is 'me' suffers. And taking this a step further, the orchestra of creation itself is affected.

The art of a crystal healer is to lend a hand so that the energy flow within our surroundings and within us is unhindered and free.

Crystals come into this because they are natural tuners and harmonisers. Each crystal has its own unique vibration. These act in the same way that a tuning fork works with a violin string.

As the struck fork makes the violin string vibrate in harmony, so crystals make chakras vibrate in sympathetic harmony.

Taking this beautiful analogy further, we know that there are different tuning forks for different strings. It is the same for chakras - different crystals for different energy centres.

Acquiring crystals

One of the most pleasurable activities in the life of a crystal healer is the finding of new crystals.

> All things being equal, in a synchronistic world, it is the crystal that chooses you. *Kal, UK*

Gifts

In one sense it is better if the crystal 'finds' you. By this I mean crystals that have been given to you, as gifts perhaps, are a good source for healing crystals.

> A great way to acquire crystals as gifts is to let your friends and family know that they are of interest to you. Suddenly you find crystals in birthday and holiday gifts. *Andre, Greece*

Nature

Finding crystals in their natural environment is an excellent method of building a healing crystal tool set. Crystals found in this way are the purest, since they have not felt the touch of others.

Scanning

This method involves laying a selection of crystals out in front of you. Once done, give your hands a shake to release any blocked energy.

Now move your hands over the crystals. If you are left-handed, use your right hand and vice versa. Should a crystal be 'yours' then you may feel one of the following sensations:

- ❑ Heat emanation
- ❑ A burst of energy (like an electrical charge)
- ❑ Tingling in fingers
- ❑ A pulse or vibration
- ❑ An inner knowledge
- ❑ Cold energy
- ❑ A shiver down your spine.

Others have felt different sensations. Try it a few times and you will become aware of 'the feeling' that is right for you.

> I love selecting crystals. I can tell which ones are for me because I get a tingle in my little finger. Isn't that odd? *Jenny, USA*

Losing your crystals

There may come a time when crystals are lost, misplaced or, indeed, 'hidden'.

It is in the nature of the universe to be in tune with you and so should the need for a crystal not be immediate, then it may well 'vanish' from your sight only to return again when it is needed.

> I have about forty crystals of various types laid out in a shallow tray. At the conclusion (and sometimes at the beginning) of a healing session, I ask my client to scan over them and they get to keep any that they tune in to – no charge! *Jaznia, USA*

Note: when giving crystals, always give a small note with them advising on use and cleansing.

Cleansing

Crystals are exchangers of energy. Wherever they are placed they take in negative energy and emit positive energy.

However once 'filled', crystals will begin to radiate negative energy and hence it is essential that crystals are regularly cleansed.

> Crystals that have picked up negative energy can pass this on, so it is important to purify newly acquired or 'used' crystals. *Andy, UK*

How often?

Newly acquired crystals should be cleansed immediately, but what about crystals that you use? Well, it depends on how often you use them. Crystals that are balancing the energy of the home or work environment should be cleansed once a fortnight.

> Don't forget the jewellery that you wear, whether it is aesthetic or for healing purposes; these should be cleansed once a week. *Delia, UK*

Crystals used in healing layouts should be cleansed immediately after use. Those that are stored away in some safe place should be cleansed once every three months.

Purification and energising

The ritual of cleansing is fairly straightforward and in most cases uncomplicated. There are several ways in which a crystal can be purified. Some purification rituals take hours, whilst others only take a few minutes. Go with what feels right is my advice.

Bright column of energy

A simple but highly effective way of cleansing a crystal is to visualise a column of bright white, golden, or amber light falling upon it. Keep this image in mind until the crystal radiates again.

Flowing water

Another equally simple method is to immerse the crystal in running (preferably flowing) water. A waterfall is ideal; however, a kitchen tap is sufficient. Allow the crystal to dry naturally in the sun afterwards.

Sunlight

Unsurprisingly, nature has provided an excellent means of purifying and releasing negative energies from crystals.

Red, yellow and orange crystals can be 'bathed' in sunlight, whilst whiter crystals (e.g. moonstone) are more appropriately bathed in moonlight.

This method of purification is a powerful cleanser and is recommended for crystals that have been used in higher healing.

Cluster or geode

Crystals can be placed on (or in) a geode crystal. Amethyst is an excellent cleanser as is a Quartz cluster.

Remember to use one of the other purifying methods (e.g., sunlight) regularly to cleanse your geode or cluster.

Smudging

Smudging is an excellent way of cleansing a crystal, as well as cleansing a room or environment. You can smudge your stone with incense or smudge sticks such as frankincense, sandalwood, sage or cedar.

Hold the crystal in your hand and use the smudge or incense stick to circle it several times keeping the crystal in the smoke of the stick.

Moonlight

Moonlight is particularly suited to white crystals. Simply place your crystals in the garden or in a window that will get the moonlight for two hours or more and you should have a set of crystals that are fully charged and ready for use.

Intent

Finally, in all cases, when purifying your crystals it is vital that you have a focus on the purpose of your actions. Keep in mind that you are carrying out an activity for a specific purpose and your crystals will help you in all your endeavours.

Dedication of intent

Dedicating a crystal is simple. It involves holding the crystal in your hand and making the simple statement that the crystal will only be used for the highest good and purest purpose.

Here are a few dedications that people have sent in via my website.

I dedicate this crystal to love and for the universal benefit of all. *Donna, USA*

I like to hold a thought of what a crystal is going to be used for and then say with the force of intent, "As my intent, so let it be." *Sharon, Ireland*

"Isis, bring goodness of purpose and heart to this stone and its uses."
Jennifer, USA

"Hecate, aid my healing." *Shana, France*

"Crystal be good for all who come to you." *Angie, UK*

Crystal properties

In this section, I will look at the properties of several popular and easily obtainable crystals. These particular crystals have been chosen because they form the basics of a crystal healer's tool kit (images are on p16-17).

Fluorite

Change

For those who are seeking change and dynamism in their lives, fluorite is the stone for you. This bringer of 'freedom of spirit' helps users shape their lives.

Forces that control us are revealed when fluorite is used. But more importantly, this crystal helps us to dissolve and negate their influence so as to free us and allow us to continue on our path to freedom. *Lisa, UK*

Creative

Fluorite aids and encourages our creative and inventive nature.

For those who feel that 'all' doors are closed, that there is 'no way out', fluorite is an excellent stone to use in your healing work, for it helps in bringing options and alternative solutions to one's mind. *Dianne, Ireland*

Mental agility

Fluorite has an emotionally stabilising effect, helping to clear confusion and giving self-confidence. It dissolves any mental blocks and helps organisation, memory, and study. It also helps stimulate the rapid absorption of information.

Physical

Fluorite helps the regeneration of skin and mucous membranes, particularly in the respiratory tract and the lungs.

It fortifies bones and teeth, decreases adhesion and helps with posture problems. Fluorite makes us physically mobile and helps with stiffness and joint problems, including arthritis.

Moonstone

Sleeping

Sleeping can be a problem for anyone who is going through emotional issues. Moonstone is helpful for both of these conditions.

Intuition
Moonstone crystals enhance our natural mediumistic, intuitive and clairvoyant powers. During the time of the full moon they can have a profound effect on our ability for lucid dreaming.

Dreams
Moonstone improves our ability to recall dreams as well as enhancing our understanding and interpretation of them, particularly lucid dreams.

For those who walk or talk in their sleep, moonstone is an excellent choice.
Angie, UK

Synchronicity
Moonstone is a remover of inhibitions and can lead one into sudden and irrational impulses. In this regard, it encourages synchronistic events in our lives, but may also lead us to trip up on our own illusions.

Feminine complaints
Moonstone can help in stimulating the pineal gland and so improves our internal hormone balance with nature's rhythms.

Menstrual and fertility problems are helped by the use of moonstone, as are afterbirth and menopausal difficulties. Indeed, the moonstone is good for all feminine complaints or hormonal fluctuations.

If you have suffered a difficult separation with a long-term partner, then, ladies, sleep with a moonstone on your right side and a rose quartz on your left. Gents reverse this layout. *Paula, USA*

Moonstone is an excellent emotional stabiliser and is particularly effective with issues of the heart when combined with rose quartz.

Bloodstone

Blood
As the name suggests this stone is a master of healing blood related problems, through its ability to toughen and oxygenate the bloodstream.

In Native American Indian healing ceremonies, bloodstones have been used to heal complaints associated with the liver. *Sara, UK*

It is also effective against disorders related to the heart, spleen, bone marrow and iron deficiencies.

Talent

The bloodstone is excellent for those wishing to be inspired, creative and intuitive. In this regard it also helps build self-confidence.

I have heard tell that the bloodstone increases intuitive ability such that knowledge about the world flows freely from one's pen. *Mariam, India*

Emotional hurt

The bloodstone is a healer of the heart in a physical and emotional sense. Thus it is good for those who have suffered hurts on an emotional level, for example, the loss of a loved one.

Mental

For those wishing to overcome distress and anxiety or who are dealing with mental disorders, the bloodstone is an excellent choice.

When wearing a bloodstone, it is best to wear it next to the skin as this facilitates the energy balance. It will, of course, work if worn over clothing, but doing so means it will take longer to feel its effects. *Sol, USA*

Oracle

The bloodstone has been known to have the ability to aid in prediction and fortune telling.

Sleep

The bloodstone aids restful slumber. A good way to activate this feature is to place one in a small bowl of water by your bedside.

Amethyst *Blue lace agate* *Citrine* *Fluorite*

Carnelian *Bloodstone* *Haematite* *Lapis lazuli*

Malachite

Moonstone

Red jasper

Black tourmaline

Green aventurine

Rose quartz

Malachite

Adventure

Truly, malachite is a stone that is for the adventurous spirit. Although lapis lazuli has similar qualities, malachite is adventure par excellence.

If you love risk and the company of lady luck, put a malachite crystal in your left pocket and see where it takes you.

Artistic appreciation

Malachite encourages an appreciation of aesthetics, sensuality and beauty. In this regard, it helps us to become closer to nature and to see beauty and patterns in all things.

Malachite awakens the desire to learn and seek knowledge. It helps us to experience life more intensely and brings forth an adventurous spirit.
Carmen, Texas

Stimulation

Malachite stimulates our inner imagery, which brings to life our dreams, imagination and memories. Old pains and traumas are brought to the fore and if we have the courage to face them, they are quietly, gently dissolved.

I recommend malachite to those who are looking to improve their dreaming and seer work. *Angela, SA*

Heart chakra

Malachite is a stone that bridges the energy of the heart and root chakras.

It is particularly useful for balancing and clearing the heart chakra. As such, it helps balance love, romance and one's own wellness.

> Malachite is a stone for the indecisive. If you find it difficult to make decisions then use malachite in your healing. This stone helps us to see clearly our options and also brings decisive action into our hands. *Donna, UK*

For the ladies
Malachite helps relieve cramps, menstruation problems and labour pains. It is also believed to encourage the development of the female sexual organs and help with sexual problems.

Some notes
Malachite is toxic and should only be used in tumbled form. It is not recommended as a gem elixir. Do not use salt to cleanse it. Indeed, the best way of cleansing is to leave it on a quartz cluster in radiant sunlight.

Tourmaline

Scrying
This stone is favoured by shamans for several reasons, one of the main being its aid in scrying rituals.

> When following my shamanistic path I always have a tourmaline to hand because it is a protective stone and ensures my protection when in the midst of ritual and spell work. *Sara, UK*

Garden
Tourmaline is an excellent stone for use in gardens and with plants of all kinds. It aids in cleansing the environment and bringing healing energy to plant life. It also acts as a pesticide and is good for removing plant pests.

Self-awareness
Tourmaline encourages us to seek and gain self-awareness. It also helps us to come to terms with what we find when looking inwards. Inspiration and compassion, as well as tolerance, are words that are associated with the energies of tourmaline crystals.

Mental
Tourmaline is a powerful mental healer and has the ability to bring creative and logical thought together. It clarifies confusion and clears up mysteries. Intuition becomes a true force in your life when using tourmaline crystals.

Paranoia is a condition that is helped by tourmaline, as are feelings of victimisation and fear. *Doreen, Canada*

Psychic attacks

Black tourmaline crystals repel dark spells, ill intent, the evil eye and negative energies. Indeed, in milder cases, the energy is transmuted into positive energy.

Healers

Most healers have a store of Tourmaline handy because it is a stone that stimulates altruism and practical creativity in healing.

Physically

Tourmaline, in particular black Tourmaline, is helpful in fighting diseases of all kinds, especially colds and flu. It also has a strengthening effect on the immune system.

Tourmaline is good for bone-related illnesses, such as arthritis and spinal problems.

Haematite

Survival

Haematite is the survivor's stone. If you are anticipating difficulties ahead then this stone is a must for your pocket. It is a stone that can lead you out of difficult situations, and is particularly good for those going through transitional times, such as a house move or separation.

Basic survival needs are maintained and enhanced by the use of haematite. In situations of fight or flight, haematite brings intuitive knowledge to bear so that the user makes the right choice. *Daniella, DC*

Willpower

For those seeking stern resolve and discipline in making changes in their life, the haematite is known for its ability to strengthen the will and help towards making headway in fulfilling ones desires.

Blood

Haematite is known for its aid in problems related to blood; for example, it is a good stone to use in issues to do with absorption, circulation and the immune system.

Grounding
Perhaps one of the best stones for grounding, haematite is an excellent stone to use in deep and long meditations.

Haematite is my favourite stone for meditation in the evening, I use it regularly for its calming and soothing effects. Combined with a singing bowl, it brings a sense of connection with the earth. *Sharon, UK*

Unwinding
If you have had a long, hard day, then haematite can bring a calm, de-stressing and relaxing state, restoring your energies and unwinding your tensions to bring a rest filled seep.

Amethyst

Spirituality
Amethyst encourages constant spiritual wakefulness, a sense of spirituality and insight into the realms of the spirit.

Wisdom
For those seeking a connection with their inner intuitive nature, use of an amethyst crystal in their meditation sessions will help.

This stone will help you reach a deep, calm state that will allow knowledge to be passed from your inner core to the conscious self.

I find using an amethyst palm crystal helpful when I am meditating on learning about the dreams that I have had. *Cathy, UK*

Support
Amethyst is a supporting crystal when it comes to those who need an aid during times of grief or loss. Sadness is allowed to fade into understanding when the amethyst is used in healing sessions.

I am a healer and a scryer of fortunes. I would recommend that one keep an amethyst or two in close proximity of scrying and divination tools, e.g., tarot cards, as this will exude positive energy into them. *Aurora, Slovenia*

Use
Placing an amethyst under your pillow will bring about a period of intense dreaming, which will bring to the fore any unresolved issues.

Once these issues are dealt with and set aside, the amethyst will encourage a deep, relaxed, refreshing and uncluttered sleep.

I am an artist as well as an amateur healer; I have found that the amethyst is a particularly useful stone for stimulating the muse and getting my inspirational juices flowing. *Fran, GA*

Sobriety
The amethyst is a crystal that helps us face up to our experiences, be they good or bad. It encourages us to deal with these issues and strengthens and nurtures our self-belief during such times.

Addictive
Amethyst enhances our capacity for concentration and effectiveness of thinking; this, in turn, helps in dealing with and overcoming blocks, controlling mechanisms, and addictive behaviours.

Headaches
Amethyst is a good stone for releasing headaches, particularly those caused by tension and anxiety. It also helps with pain in general and is useful for injuries, bruises, and swellings.

Lapis lazuli

Adventurous
Those seeking strength, both inner and outer, to change their lives are best seeking the benefits of the lapis lazuli crystal. This crystal is the stone for the adventurous *seeker* spirit.

Wisdom and honesty
Lapis lazuli is a brilliant stone for bestowing wisdom and honesty and is a crucial stone when it comes to seeking inner truths.

Lapis is a stone that allows us to be ourselves and provides an energy that liberates us from compromises and holding back.

Often the lapis has been known as the 'stone of friendship'. Those who are seeking friends and companions should look to this stone. *Sally, Italy*

Interactions
Lapis encourages us to seek company and interactions with others; furthermore, it helps communication and brings clarity to us when we are conveying feelings and emotions.

Honour
Lapis is a stone that helps bring out honourable traits. For example, it brings to the fore: dignity, honesty, and uprightness.

One of my favourite stones is the lapis lazuli, I have heard it called the 'noble stone' and that is how I see it. *Andrea, UK*

Mystical
For those who are seeking a more spiritual and mystical path in life, I advise you to court the lapis lazuli.

Physically
Lapis helps with issues relating to the neck, larynx, and vocal chords, particularly if they originate in reserved or repressed anger.

Blue lace agate

Cooling
Blue lace is a beautifully crafted (by nature) stone. It has an extraordinary ability to calm and soothe the mind as well as cool down 'hot' heads. It brings peace of mind in troubled times.

Blue lace is definitely my favourite stone. I have it all over my house and cannot get enough of it. It is calming, relaxing and beautiful to look at.
Kal, UK

Expression
When used on the throat chakra, this stone helps the wearer to communicate freely and without confusion. The wearer is able to convey feelings and thoughts with a freedom from embarrassment or nervousness.

My husband started a new job in which he had to give a lot of presentations. Initially, he was very nervous and felt that his words flowed too fast and were not received well. I gave him a blue lace pendant to wear and slowly his confidence returned. Now he actually enjoys giving presentations.
Gaynor, SC

Rejection

Some people often feel rejected. Whether this is because of real or imagined perceptions, the Blue lace agate is a stone that can help.

It is also useful for those who fear being judged (which again is a fear of rejection). The blue lace is a gentle stone that can dissolve such concerns, leaving one feeling refreshed and ready to take on the challenges of life.

Strangely, I have had clients who are the opposite; by this I mean that they fear success. For such conditions I also recommend blue lace agate stones.
Sylvia, Geneva

Physically

Blue lace is a healer of conditions associated with the throat chakra. Thus, conditions relating to the shoulders, neck, thyroid, and lymphatic system are all helped by blue lace agates.

The blue lace agate also relieves fevers and nervous system complaints and reinforces bone and skeletal structures.

Diabetics often have a condition called burning hands or feet, in which their hands and feet feel like they are on fire, particularly during the night. For such conditions I highly recommend a blue lace palm stone held in the palm when going to sleep. *Petra, UK*

Rose quartz

Ladies

For ladies who are seeking relaxation and calmness, particularly from emotional issues, rose quartz crystals are of great benefit.

Gentle

The rose quartz makes us gentle, yet firm. There is no question of pliability or giving in. Rather, there is an awareness of the gentle soft nature overcoming the hard strong one.

When thinking or describing the rose quartz I like to mention the old Chinese saying, "Become like water." This, I feel, is what the rose quartz is about.
Julia, Argentina

Compassion

Rose Quartz helps us to help others; it encourages helpfulness, openness and the desire for a pleasant ambience.

Sensitivity
Empathy and compassion are two words that are synonymous with rose quartz. With these comes a, often, overwhelming emotion of sensitivity.

Romance
The rose quartz is famed for its romantic and loving nature. It is a stone that is ideal for bringing out loving emotions.

Depth
Often issues that have been buried for many years cause problems for us today, mostly on a subconscious level. Rose quartz is a stone that can help to bring such issue to the surface. It is a great stone for delving deep within us to uncover lost issues that need to be resolved before we can grow and move on.

Forgiveness
Coupled with the ability to bring buried issues to the fore is the faculty to bring us the peace of forgiveness.

Forgiveness of others is a powerfully liberating force. Rose quartz is a stone that can bring this out in us. *Agueda, Spain*

Fertility
Rose quartz is a stone that helps with sexual problems and encourages fertility.

Green aventurine

Luck
The aventurine is known as the 'gamblers' stone' in some circles as it is the bringer of good fortune. With this is coupled the ability to confer an unusually high sense of self-confidence, which one must be wary of.

Independence, self-confidence, happiness and leadership are all qualities I associate with the aventurine crystal. *John, DC*

Skin
The anti-inflammatory properties of the aventurine make it an ideal stone for those suffering from skin diseases, skin eruptions and allergies. It also fortifies the connective tissues.

Heart
The aventurine is a healer and protector of the heart, it is a stone that encourages regeneration of the heart, stimulates the fat metabolism and lowers cholesterol levels.

The aventurine enhances creativity and motivation, particularly if these are focused on issues related to the heart or love. *Georgina, London*

Those who seek to persevere in a task or endeavour, for example, quitting smoking or moving on in a relationship should try wearing an aventurine pendant. *Jan, Dublin*

Green fingers
Green aventurine is often called the 'gardener's' stone, as it is a stone that brings health and vitality to flora and fauna.

Place a green aventurine in each of the four corners of your garden and watch it flourish. *Claire, ZM*

Environment
The aventurine is an excellent environmental cleanser, particularly when placed near computers, televisions or indeed any electronic appliance.

For mobile phones I recommend a small aventurine stone on a key ring to dissipate the emissions. *Angela, Italy*

Citrine

Happy stone
The citrine is often called the 'happy stone' and is remarkable in that it is continuously energised, meaning it never needs to be cleansed.

Self-confidence
Citrine encourages individuality, self-confidence and the courage to face and enjoy life. For some, feelings of guilt detract from their enjoyment of life; they have a feeling that they should not or do not deserve to enjoy life. If this is you then the citrine is a stone that can help.

If you are wondering why you are not happy when there is nothing for you to be sad about, the citrine is for you. *Delia, UK*

Variety
The citrine encourages a change of pace in life, bringing a sense of dynamism and movement into life. New experiences, variety and self-realisation are the order of the day when the citrine is around.

The citrine is a wonderful stone for getting the creative juices flowing. I am a painter by night and potter by day. In both cases I have plenty of citrine clusters around me to keep my work original and continuous. *Rahul, Turkey*

Self-expression
Extroversion is the characteristic often defined by the citrine, coupling this with an encouragement towards artistic and creative endeavours.

Those who wish to unleash the muse that is trapped within them should try wearing a citrine bracelet or ring. *Angie, CA*

Positive attitude
The citrine encourages a positive attitude in several ways. One is to bring about a feeling of optimism, another is to bring an understanding of situations, and a third is to stimulate Lady Luck in your life.

Self-healing
The citrine helps us digest impressions we have received, stimulates the ability to comfort and helps us overcome depression and free ourselves from negative influences.

Physically
The citrine is good for conditions relating to the spleen, stomach, and pancreas (in particular diabetes). It also has a cleansing action on the blood, helping to detoxify it.

Carnelian

Anchor
The carnelian is an excellent stone for providing stability. It is well known for its 'feet on the ground' nature. Saying this, it is also good for providing energy, vitality and motivation, particularly in creative pursuits, 'acting' being an excellent example.

Cycle
We are within a cycle of life, death and life again; the carnelian brings an understanding and acceptance of this cycle, allowing us to use this knowledge to bring serenity and peace into our lives.

Shamans have used carnelians in their journeys beyond this life as both guides and protectors. *Sara, UK*

Self-awareness

The carnelian can be of great benefit when acquiring self-knowledge. It is a stone that helps you understand your inner workings. It overcomes negative conditioning and encourages steadfastness whilst promoting analytical abilities and clarifying perceptions.

I have also found the carnelian to be a life-changing stone; it made difficult decisions easy by putting priorities into perspective. *Kal, UK*

Metabolism

Rarely is a stone found that can shake the metabolism into full working order. Carnelian is filled with vigour and energy, so in most cases it has no difficulty in stimulating the metabolism.

Healing

Problems to do with rheumatism, arthritis, neuralgia and the lower back are all helped by the use of the carnelian.

Carnelian, particularly the red one, is a warming stone and can help with chills. *Diane, New Zealand*

Blood

The carnelian aids the absorption of nutrients into the blood, for example, vitamins and minerals. It also ensures that a good supply of blood is maintained to the organs and tissues.

Red jasper

Times of stress

If you are going through difficult times or stressful periods, for example, separation from a partner, deadlines at work or exams, use of the jasper crystal is highly recommended. This crystal is a bringer of tranquillity and calmness. It supports the user through trying times by creating a sense of peace and serenity.

Jasper makes an ideal gift for those who are hospitalised. Firstly, it protects from any contagions that may be floating freely. Also it is an energiser of the body's immune system. *Randy, USA*

Dreams

Jasper is a good stone for those who wish to work with their dreams. If you are having problems recalling your dreams, then try laying a jasper crystal by the side of your bed.

Shamans use jasper crystals when they wish to go on safe and protected astral or dream journeys. Place them in a pentacle shape around your bed or sleeping area. *Sara, UK*

Action

Jasper is a stone that promotes action. Those who are given to excessive procrastination should try wearing a jasper pendant. So should those who have ideas but need to be stimulated into action.

A friend of mine wanted to know if there was a crystal that she could wear to help motivate her to lose weight. I recommended a jasper brooch that she could clip to her belt (root and sacral), as this stone makes one determined. *Keith, UAE*

Physically

Jasper aids the digestive and sexual regions of the body. In particular, if you are suffering from trapped wind then try placing a jasper crystal over the stomach.

Jasper makes an excellent 'worry' bead. *Jan, Dublin*

Justice

Jasper, the red one in particular, is a great stone for righting wrongs. Its talents include reversing unfair judgments and helping one fight the 'good fight'.

Foresee

Jasper has a sense of the future, in that it is able to foresee upcoming issues and place solutions within the grasp of the user. It is a great synchronicity enhancer in this regard.

Layouts

Layouts are, as the name suggests, the ways in which crystals are laid out to heal. Crystals can be laid on a person, around a person or in an environment.

How long should crystals be placed?

Crystals begin to work instantaneously; hence, it is difficult to come up with a reason as to why they should be placed in a layout for long periods of time. I suggest no more than twenty minutes for each layout.

An exception to this is when doing meditations using crystals. In this case leave them in place for as long as required.

Size of crystals

Crystals work on a vibrational and energetic level. The size of a crystal does not, in my view, make a difference to the effectiveness of the stone. Most healers agree, however, that cracked or damaged crystals are less potent than undamaged ones.

Intuition

You will find information concerning crystal healing in books, on the Internet, from teachers and from healers. Always give a good amount of consideration to your intuition.

Caution

If at any time you feel uncomfortable with a crystal, don't use it. Sensations are important when dealing with crystals so pay attention to them.

Laying crystals on others

It is absolutely essential that you get feedback from your clients as you are treating them. After laying each crystal, ask them how they feel, whether they are uncomfortable or okay. Also, stay with them during the whole treatment.

Chakra-balancing layout

A chakra balance is simple to perform and brings together the colours associated with chakras and the colours of crystals.

For this layout eight crystals are required. These are black tourmaline, red jasper, carnelian, citrine, rose quartz, blue lace agate, lapis lazuli and amethyst.

The black tourmaline is used as a grounding crystal and ensures that you remain level headed and focused during the balance.

Sit down on the floor or bed and place the tourmaline between your feet. Now lie down and place the crystals as follows:

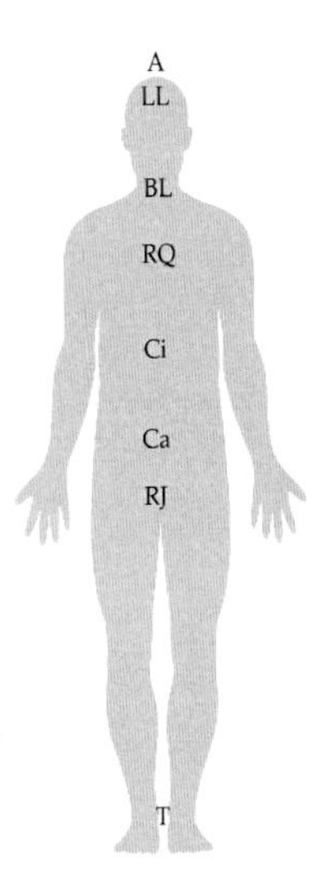

Crystal layout

Red jasper on the root chakra, carnelian on the sacral, citrine on the solar plexus, rose quartz on the heart, blue lace on the throat chakra, lapis on the brow and amethyst on the crown.

As you place each crystal wait a few seconds for its presence to settle. If you feel uncomfortable with any crystal then remove it.

You can keep the layout in place for as long as you 'feel' is necessary, but this should not be more than around twenty minutes.

A variation on the chakra balance layout is to first determine any chakras that are misaligned using a pendulum (see later) and then just work on those.

New-beginnings layout

This is a wonderful layout for those who are starting out in a new enterprise, whether it is a house move, a new relationship, or a new job.

Here are some of the things that people consider when starting on the journey towards 'the undiscovered country.'

- ❑ Foresight of dangers
- ❑ Prosperity and success
- ❑ Intuition knowledge
- ❑ The aid of angels
- ❑ Understanding
- ❑ Luck
- ❑ Courage
- ❑ Friendship
- ❑ Self-confidence
- ❑ Vitality and energy

This layout requires a garnet, malachite, jasper, bloodstone, aquamarine, rose quartz, amethyst or quartz cluster and moonstone amulet or pendant.

Begin by placing the rose quartz over the heart (note, not the heart chakra). Now place the aquamarine over the heart chakra. The bloodstone is placed next over the throat chakra.

Place the malachite upon the solar plexus chakra and the garnet upon the sacral chakra.

Finally, place the jasper upon the root chakra and the moonstone upon the brow chakra. Note: remove the string or chain from the moonstone before use.

Leave the layout in place for about twenty minutes. Then remove the moonstone and place it on the cluster crystal. Then about every two minutes remove one of the other crystals and place it around the cluster.

Once the final crystal is removed remain prone for five or so minutes. Then take the moonstone and place it around your neck.

Meditation layout

This is a wonderful layout that helps with meditation and self-reflection. It requires five rose quartz crystals and one green aventurine. You will also require a candle.

Before beginning this meditation create five affirmations; here are some examples:

- I am becoming healthier.
- I deserve love and happiness.
- I am becoming more loving.
- The past has no power over me.
- I forgive and am forgiven.
- I release old hurt and anxiety easily.

Once you have created five affirmations, write them down on a small card or paper and you are ready to begin.

Sit in a comfortable position and place the lit candle before you. Now place the five rose quartz crystals in a circle some 10 inches wide around the candle.

Take the first affirmation in your hand and place the aventurine in the twelve o'clock position between two rose quartz crystals.

Meditate on the affirmation for five minutes taking in its meaning for you. As you do let your gaze fall upon the layout before you.

Move the aventurine along one crystal and take up the next affirmation. Continue in this way until you have completed the five affirmations.

Wearing crystals

If possible a crystal works best if it is located close to its appropriate chakra. For example, the root chakra is associated with the colour red and so a red jasper located close to this chakra would be more effective than one located further away.

Given this, blue lace agate, turquoise and topaz necklaces are an excellent healing choice, as are rose quartz or green aventurine pendants (particularly those with a long chain that reaches to the chest area).

Lapis lazuli earrings are a brilliant healing idea, as are amethyst or clear quartz hairpins.

If you are so inclined, then carnelians or citrines are good stones to have in your belly button.

Tying a red jasper crystal to your waist belt is an excellent means of energising the root chakra, as is carrying one in your trouser pocket.

Pendulum use

Using a pendulum to determine a chakra energy state is easy. The first step is to determine a yes or no response.

To do this hold the pendulum up before you and ask out loud, "Please give me a 'Yes' response." Then observe the pendulum to see what occurs. Now do the same but ask for a 'No' response.

Once this has been done you can ask about the status of any of your chakras, e.g., "Is my heart chakra balanced?"

Thank you

I hope that you have found this booklet useful and it has ignited your desire to explore the world of complementary healing and, in particular, crystal healing. Please pop along to my website and say hello.

www.healingbooks.net

Until next time,

Kal

CW00601662

Calculations for the Hotel and Catering Industry

G E Gee

Head of Department of Food and Fashion
South Downs College of Further Education
Havant Hants

Formerly Examiner in Book-keeping and Food costing
for the East Midlands Examination Union

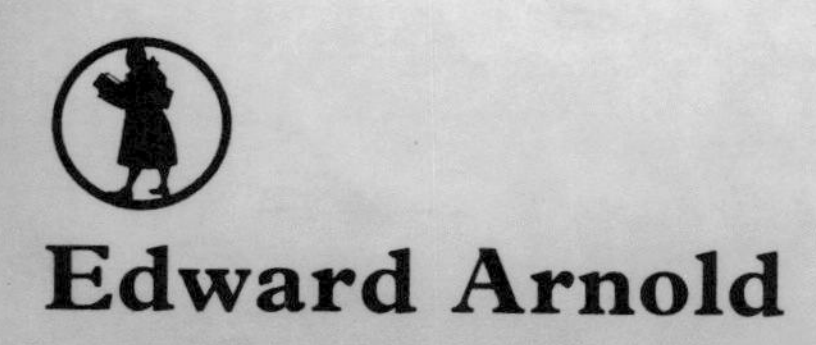

© G E Gee 1980
First published 1980
by Edward Arnold (Publishers) Ltd
41 Bedford Square London WC1B 3DQ

Edward Arnold (Australia) Pty Ltd, 80 Waverley Road, Caulfield East, Victoria 3145, Australia

Reprinted 1981, 1982, 1983, 1985, 1986

All rights reserved. No part of this publication may be reproduced, stored in a retrieval system, or transmitted in any form or by any means, electronic, mechanical, photocopying, recording or otherwise, without the prior permission of Edward Arnold (Publishers) Ltd.

British Library Cataloguing in Publication Data

Gee, G E
Calculations for the hotel and catering industry.
1. Food service – Mathematics
I. Title
642′.47′0151 TX911.3.M/

ISBN 0–7131–0414–7

Filmset in Great Britain by
Northumberland Press Ltd, Gateshead, Tyne and Wear

Printed in Hong Kong by
Wing King Tong Ltd.

Preface

In writing this book both students and lecturers have constantly been in mind. To achieve success in the Hotel and Catering Industry students need a good basic arithmetical knowledge and lecturers need many examples available to supplement their lesson notes.

This book is designed for students taking City and Guilds (Craft Catering and Hotel Reception), O.N.D., E.M.E.U. Food Costing examinations, B.T.E.C., and those working in the industry.

It is recognised that Hotel and Catering students are not always interested in mathematical topics but in times of inflation and price competition a sound knowledge of costing is essential for business survival. The book is written in non-mathematical terms to present to the student methods and facts that may have previously been difficult to understand.

Except for the past examinations questions at the back of the book, metric units are used throughout and it is hoped that students will appreciate that it is easier to use kilograms and litres in working out problems.

Value Added Tax is ignored for the greater part to enable questions concerning sales to be less complicated during the learning process.

In working through the book students and lecturers will find examples for *discussion* and it is suggested that lecturers will use these questions as a basis for group topics.

GEG

The author wishes to thank the East Midlands Educational Union for permission to use the questions from past Food Costing examination papers and congratulates this examining body for giving prominence by examination to a subject so important in the Hotel and Catering Industry.

Contents

1

Addition

We can not cost a menu, present a guest's bill, check an invoice or even work out our own wages without an ability to add.

How accurately can you add?

1.	2.	3.	4.
426	1208	3089	2464
48	875	706	38
870	99	8214	7997

5.	6.	7.	8.
702	2567	392	6443
8029	3829	452	27
1307	4776	8267	2877

The addition of decimals is treated in the same way, remembering that the first place behind the decimal point is the tenths column, the second place is the hundredths column, the third place is the thousandths etc, e.g.

14.372 is 14 whole numbers, 3 tenths, 7 hundredths and 2 thousandths.

9.	10.	11.	12.
4.82	18.72	175.3	401.72
20.54	4.3	19.82	248.03
0.45	32.0	311.08	36.54
34.74	77.07	12.75	74.58

13.	14.	15.	16.
17.27	627.34	425.38	146.27
3.05	13.2	29.72	378.72
29.77	184.17	0.37	584.47
14.23	74.23	348.27	123.97

17. £	18. £	19. £	20. £
87.32	443.08	67.85½	124.34
0.47	85.00	29.38	25.65
25.65	27.40	17.92½	308.84
1.05	18.38	74.76½	0.79

21. Kilograms (kg)	22. kg	23. Litres	24. Litres
4.25	18.75	27.34	2.47
13.37	127.32	70.45	41.74
28.75	84.55	148.25	0.88

Sometimes it is necessary to add horizontal columns of figures. For instance, Hotel Receptionists often add Tabular Ledgers in this way.

Test your skill in working out the following.

25. 4.32 + 14.74 + 30.85

26. 17.05 + 48.1 + 34.56

27. 81.63 + 24 + 321.28 + 50.67

28. £1.07 + £38.25 + £25.79

29. £100.38 + £324.07 + £528.39 + £35.00

30. £3.08 + £0.41 + £17.84 + £1.96

31. £0.74 + £0.32 + £0.47 + £0.89

32. £16.37½ + £20.48 + £8.20 + £8.34½

33. £172.38½ + £75.93 + £100.48½ + £45.88½

34. £1024.55½ + £8.05 + £527.79½ + £600.00

In some cases there is a need to give an answer to three decimal places.

½p can be written as £0.00½ or £0.005
1 gram (g) can be written as 0.001 kg
1 millilitre (ml) can be written as 0.001 litre
5 kg 225 g can be written as 5.225 kg

Write the following in kg.

35. 7 kg 425 g

36. 18 kg 350 g

37. 125 kg 25 g

38. 68 kg 5 g

3 litres 175 ml can be written as 3.175 litres

Write the following in litres.

39. 6 litres 175 ml **40.** 25 litres 340 ml

41. 130 litres 42 ml **42.** 7 litres 6 ml

43. £	**44.** £	**45.** £	**46.** £
4.127	18.34	18.205	141.255
3.038	2.278	1.005	70.185
1.245	0.045	3.128	305.295
8.005	1.36	14.00	211.384

47. kg	**48.** kg	**49.** litres	**50.** litres
40.725	21.125	17.628	65.775
128.129	39.338	50.250	20.378
0.499	8.584	49.675	71.445

2

Subtraction

1.	**2.**	**3.**	**4.**
483 –	1432 –	4156 –	7243 –
127	294	828	1738

5. £	**6.** £	**7.** £	**8.** £
17.84 –	25.62 –	306.28 –	1260.45 –
3.26	8.84	14.49	795.63

9. kg	**10.** kg	**11.** kg	**12.** kg
13.275 –	44.184 –	20.42 –	125.250 –
8.325	27.356	12.65	70.275

13. litres	**14.** litres	**15.** litres	**16.** litres
9.25 –	103.150 –	45.201 –	17.123 –
3.326	27.326	13.222	0.445

17. £18.43 – £6.28

18. £36.08 – £0.36

19. £125.37 – £84.47

20. £17.36 – £8.04½

21. £8.724 – £1.208

22. £18.364 – £17.842

23. 13.25 kg – 8.75 kg

24. 120.350 kg – 75.275 kg

25. 7.46 kg – 2.72 kg

26. 35.346 kg – 28.148 kg

27. 81.01 litres – 9.21 litres

28. 14.00 litres – 3.50 litres

29. 17.125 litres – 13.250 litres

30. 125.270 litres – 48.370 litres

31. Find the difference between £704.25 and £342.95

32. Find the difference between 4.275 kg and 1.791 kg

33. By how much is £56.07 greater than £27.39?

34. By how much is 25.5 litres greater than 4.125 litres?

3

Multiplication

To achieve success in this section, multiplication tables must be known.

Test your tables.

1. 3 × 6	**2.** 5 × 8	**3.** 7 × 4	**4.** 5 × 6
5. 9 × 8	**6.** 11 × 12	**7.** 8 × 4	**8.** 7 × 12
9. 3 × 9	**10.** 12 × 4	**11.** 9 × 9	**12.** 6 × 8
13. 11 × 11	**14.** 6 × 7	**15.** 4 × 9	**16.** 4 × 5
17. 8 × 8	**18.** 5 × 12	**19.** 6 × 6	**20.** 12 × 12

Now to use the tables.

21. 145 × 6 **22.** 367 × 7 **23.** 408 × 8

24. 125 × 32 **25.** 423 × 78 **26.** 374 × 193

In multiplying decimals, first work the sum ignoring the decimal place, e.g.

```
 7.48 ×
    6
 ----
 4488
 ----
```

Next, count the number of figures behind the decimal point in the question and place the point so that there are the same number of figures behind the point in the answer, e.g.

```
  7.48 ×
     6
 -----
 44.88
 -----
```

Here is another example.

```
 7.48 ×
 0.6
 -----
 4.488
 -----
```

N.B. the total number of figures behind the decimal point was three (4, 8, 6).

Here is an unusual example.

```
 0.47 ×
 0.12
 ------
 0.0564
 ------
```

27. 17.3 × 6 **28.** 42.31 × 8 **29.** 17.4 × 4.3

30. £5.62 × 9 **31.** £10.35 × 7 **32.** £25.36 × 5

33. £78.42 × 63 **34.** £47.71 × 84 **35.** £30.28 × 2.5

36. £4.275 × 8 **37.** £14.128 × 13 **38.** £8.493 × 124

39. £1.25½ × 4 **40.** £10.35½ × 9 **41.** £2.60½ × 13

42. 6.275 kg × 5 **43.** 1.476 kg × 12 **44.** 13.75 kg × 15

45. 102.5 kg × 27 46. 14.38 kg × 42 47. 72.125 kg × 56

48. 13.5 litres × 9 49. 2.65 litres × 21 50. 62.5 litres × 2.5

Quick Methods

17.32 × 10 = 173.2
14.25 × 100 = 1425
25.63 × 1000 = 25 630

Note that the decimal point is moved one place to the right when multiplying by 10, two places when multiplying by 100, three places when multiplying by 1000 and so on.

£14.34 × 100 = £1434.00
£3.72 × 10 = £37.20
6.75 kg × 10 = 67.5 kg
17.5 litres × 100 = 1750 litres

Try these using the quick method.

51. £4.32 × 10 52. £14.65 × 100 53. £0.14 × 1000

54. 5.64 kg × 10 55. 21.05 litres × 100 56. 16.125 kg × 1000

4 Division

Again it is important to know the tables.

1. 72 ÷ 9 2. 144 ÷ 12 3. 30 ÷ 6 4. 56 ÷ 7

5. 54 ÷ 9 6. 48 ÷ 6 7. 120 ÷ 12 8. 45 ÷ 5

9. 72 ÷ 12 10. 27 ÷ 3 11. 42 ÷ 6 12. 63 ÷ 7

13. 121 ÷ 11 14. 49 ÷ 7 15. 36 ÷ 12 16. 35 ÷ 5

17. 36 ÷ 6 18. 81 ÷ 9 19. 60 ÷ 12 20. 28 ÷ 4

Using the tables.

21. $824 \div 4$ **22.** $2545 \div 5$ **23.** $876 \div 6$

24. $4131 \div 9$ **25.** $3528 \div 7$ **26.** $780 \div 12$

27. $33\,640 \div 8$ **28.** $8041 \div 11$ **29.** $2385 \div 9$

A common error in division is to forget the 0 in the answer to the following type of example.

$$\begin{array}{r} 1406 \\ 6\overline{)8436} \end{array}$$

Be careful in working out these questions.

30. $2427 \div 3$ **31.** $545 \div 5$ **32.** $34\,812 \div 12$

It is worthwhile revising the set out of a long division sum.

$$\begin{array}{r} 234 \\ 34\overline{)7956} \\ \underline{68} \\ 115 \\ \underline{102} \\ 136 \\ \underline{136} \end{array}$$

a Having decided 34 divides into 79 two times put the 2 in the answer over the 9 and the 68 (2 × 34) under the 79 and subtract to find the 11 remainder.

b Keep the figures in the correct column and bring the 5 vertically down to make 115.

c Having decided 34 divides into 115 three times, put the 3 in answer over the 5 and the 102 (3 × 34) under the 115 and subtract to find the 13 remainder.

d Keep the figures in the correct column and bring the 6 vertically down to make 136.

e Having decided 34 divides into 136 four times, put the 4 over the 6 and the 136 under the 136 and subtract to find there is no remainder.

33. $425 \div 25$ **34.** $5550 \div 30$ **35.** $3504 \div 48$

In decimal division the following points should be observed:

a First place the decimal point in the answer vertically above the decimal point in the question, e.g.

$$\begin{array}{r} . \\ 7\overline{)31.5} \end{array}$$

and then divide:

$$\begin{array}{r} 4.5 \\ 7\overline{)31.5} \end{array}$$

36. 33.2 ÷ 8 **37.** 16.86 ÷ 6 **38.** 61.5 ÷ 3

b Do not divide by a decimal, e.g.

$$3.2\overline{)22.4}$$

Multiply both the divisor (3.2) and the dividend (22.4) by 10 and the sum now becomes

$$32\overline{)224}$$

Similarly

$$0.25\overline{)1.475}$$

becomes

$$25\overline{)147.5}\ \text{(by multiplying by 100)}$$

39. 86.1 ÷ 0.7 **40.** 3.84 ÷ 0.12 **41.** 0.375 ÷ 0.25

c By adding a 0 to any remainder and dividing again a more accurate answer to a third decimal place can be obtained, e.g.

$$5\overline{)12.34}$$

answer

$$\begin{array}{r} 2.468 \\ 5\overline{)12.340} \end{array}$$

$$4\overline{)34.1}$$

answer

$$\begin{array}{r} 8.525 \\ 4\overline{)34.100} \end{array}$$

42. 63.1 ÷ 5 **43.** 5.39 ÷ 4 **44.** 35.6 ÷ 8

More practice in division.

45. 17.12 ÷ 8 **46.** 4.068 ÷ 9 **47.** 37.125 ÷ 25

48. 1.72 ÷ 0.4 **49.** 15.48 ÷ 1.2 **50.** 2.655 ÷ 0.15

51. 46.21 ÷ 5 **52.** 7.86 ÷ 12 **53.** 28.4 ÷ 16

54. £15.24 ÷ 6 **55.** 32.494 kg ÷ 7 **56.** £104.58 ÷ 42

57. £51.30 ÷ 4 **58.** 15.738 litres ÷ 6 **59.** £1136.20 ÷ 52

Sometimes an answer is required worked out to a certain number of places after the decimal point, e.g.

$$143.1 \div 8$$

Give the answer to 2 decimal places.

$$\begin{array}{r} 17.88 \\ 8\overline{)143.10} \end{array}$$

Ignore any remainder (in this case 6) after 2 decimal places.

60. $37.45 \div 6$ (answer to 2 decimal places)

61. £14.75 ÷ 9 (answer to 3 decimal places)

62. 17.5 kg ÷ 4 (answer to 2 decimal places)

A more accurate answer can be obtained by *correcting* to a given number of decimal places, e.g.

Express 17.378 corrected to 2 decimal places.

Method

Examine the figure in the third decimal place and if the figure is 5 or a higher value (in this case it is 8) then add 1 to the value of the figure in the second decimal place. If the figure is lower than 5, leave the figure in the second decimal place unchanged.

17.378 corrected to 2 decimal places is 17.38

Remember, examine the figure in the second decimal place if you are correcting to 1 decimal place, examine the figure in the third decimal place if you are correcting to 2 decimal places and so on.

Here are more examples:

1.32651 corrected to 3 decimal places is 1.327
14.183 corrected to 2 decimal places is 14.18
£405.426 to the nearest penny is £405.43

63. 14.295 corrected to 1 decimal place

64. 1.8272 to 3 decimal places.

65. 18.4971 corrected to 3 decimal places

66. £49.128 to the nearest penny.

67. 21.775 kg to the nearest kg

68. $143.5 \div 8$ corrected to 2 decimal places.

69. $13.3 \div 4$ corrected to 2 decimal places

70. £45.27 ÷ 7 corrected to 3 decimal places.

Quick Methods

$421.7 \div 10 = 42.17$
$118.4 \div 100 = 1.184$
$1423 \div 1000 = 1.423$

The decimal point is moved one place to the left when dividing by 10, two places when dividing by 100, three places when dividing by 1000 and so on.

71. $14.32 \div 10$

72. £36.42 ÷ 100

73. £11 236.00 ÷ 100

74. 45 kg ÷ 10

75. 410.3 litres ÷ 100

76. 525 litres ÷ 1000

5

Problems using the four rules

1. Find the price of each item and total the bill.
4 kg of butter at £2.25 per kg
8 kg of sugar at £0.30 per kg
2.5 kg of flour at £0.23 per kg
100 g ground ginger at £3.10 per kg
3 litres of vinegar at £0.21 per litre

2. The ingredient costs in producing 2000 cups of tea are as follows:
Tea—3.75 kg at £0.64 per kg
Milk—8 litres at £0.27 per litre
Sugar—19 kg at £0.30 per kg
Find the profit made per cup if tea is sold at 10p per cup (answer to nearest $\frac{1}{2}$p).

3. The total food cost to produce 25 covers was £19.20. Calculate the cost per cover **a** to 2 decimal places of £1 **b** corrected to decimal places of £1.

4. The costs in producing a dinner for 50 guests were as follows:
Food costs per cover £1.09
Wages £38.50
Other costs £43.00
If the charge for the dinner was £3.25 per head, calculate the total profit made by the hotel.

5. **a** Find the cost of making 1000 cakes at £0.045 each.
b 100 cups of coffee were sold for £15.00. Find the charge per cup.

6. If 28 portions can be obtained from a turkey, how many turkeys should be ordered if 400 portions are required to be served?

7. How many 50 g portions of peas can be served from a 10 kg packet?

6

Fractions

Cancelling

Whilst it is true to say that a correct answer in fractions and percentages can be obtained without cancelling, it is also true that cancelling at the right time makes the work simpler and quicker.

The principle of cancelling is easy to understand.

This fraction means that the 2 is being divided by 4.

$$\frac{2}{4}$$

By dividing the top *and* bottom lines by 2 the fraction becomes $\frac{1}{2}$

$$\frac{2}{4} = \frac{1}{2}$$

The fraction $\frac{2}{4}$ has been divided top and bottom by 2 and becomes $\frac{1}{2}$ but the value has remained the same (two quarters are the same value as one half).

The secret is in finding a number that will divide *exactly* into *both* the top and bottom lines.

Examples

a Cancel $\frac{20}{35}$

$\frac{20}{35} = \frac{4}{7}$ (By dividing top and bottom line by 5)

b Cancel $\frac{125}{1000}$

$\frac{125}{1000} = \frac{1}{8}$ (Divide by 125)

Cancel the following:

1. $\frac{40}{45}$ **2.** $\frac{18}{36}$ **3.** $\frac{42}{54}$ **4.** $\frac{108}{144}$

5. $\frac{70}{120}$ **6.** $\frac{4}{12}$ **7.** $\frac{28}{35}$ **8.** $\frac{6}{24}$

9. $\frac{75}{100}$ **10.** $\frac{16}{64}$ **11.** $\frac{17}{51}$ **12.** $\frac{4000}{5000}$

7

Mixed numbers and improper fractions

Before percentages can be worked out successfully you should know how to multiply fractions and that involves mixed numbers and improper fractions.

Example

a Change $5\frac{1}{4}$ to quarters.
(in mathematical terms the mixed number $5\frac{1}{4}$ is to be changed to an improper fraction.)

Method

In 5 whole numbers there are 20 quarters (5×4)
Therefore in $5\frac{1}{4}$ there are 21 quarters $= \frac{21}{4}$ (An improper fraction)

b Change the mixed number $3\frac{2}{5}$ to fifths.

Method

In 3 whole numbers there are 15 fifths $= \frac{15}{5}$
Therefore in $3\frac{2}{5}$ there are $\frac{17}{5}$

1. Change $4\frac{1}{2}$ to halves
2. Change $2\frac{2}{5}$ to fifths
3. Change $7\frac{1}{4}$ to quarters
4. Change $5\frac{5}{6}$ to sixths
5. Change $10\frac{2}{3}$ to thirds
6. Change $1\frac{14}{15}$ to fifteenths
7. Change $3\frac{3}{4}$ to quarters
8. Change $2\frac{2}{7}$ to sevenths
9. Change $4\frac{3}{8}$ to eighths
10. Change $20\frac{3}{10}$ to tenths

Changing to mixed numbers.

Example

Change the improper fraction $\frac{20}{3}$ to a mixed number.

Method

Divide 20 by 3 = 6 whole numbers, remainder 2 thirds.
Answer $6\frac{2}{3}$

Change to mixed numbers.

11. $\frac{7}{6}$ **12.** $\frac{8}{3}$ **13.** $\frac{25}{8}$

14. $\frac{24}{11}$ **15.** $\frac{100}{9}$ **16.** $\frac{29}{7}$

17. $\frac{5}{2}$ **18.** $\frac{51}{5}$ **19.** $\frac{39}{6}$ (Cancel first)

20. $\frac{18}{8}$ (Cancel first) **21.** $\frac{100}{12}$ (Cancel first) **22.** $\frac{20}{6}$ (Cancel first)

8

Multiplication of fractions

Example

a $\frac{2}{3} \times \frac{4}{5}$

Multiply top line, multiply bottom line

$\frac{2}{3} \times \frac{4}{5} = \frac{8}{15}$

b $\frac{2}{3} \times \frac{6}{7}$

By cancelling, the sum is easier to work out.

$$\frac{2}{\cancel{3}_1} \times \frac{\cancel{6}^2}{7} = \frac{4}{7}$$

Remember, whatever number is divided into the top line must also be divided into the bottom line. (In the above example the division is by 3.)

c $4\frac{1}{2} \times \frac{3}{4}$

Change all mixed numbers to improper fractions before multiplying.

$$\frac{9}{2} \times \frac{3}{4} = \frac{27}{8} = 3\tfrac{3}{8}$$

Multiply the following:

1. $\frac{3}{5} \times \frac{4}{7}$	**11.** $1\frac{1}{2} \times 1\frac{2}{3}$
2. $\frac{5}{8} \times \frac{5}{6}$	**12.** $2\frac{1}{2} \times 2\frac{1}{3}$
3. $\frac{2}{7} \times \frac{3}{4}$	**13.** $2\frac{2}{3} \times 5$ (Write 5 as $\frac{5}{1}$)
4. $\frac{6}{11} \times \frac{2}{3}$	**14.** $3\frac{1}{4} \times 8$
5. $\frac{1}{2} \times 3\frac{2}{3}$	**15.** $6 \times \frac{2}{3}$
6. $2\frac{1}{2} \times \frac{3}{7}$	**16.** $2\frac{3}{5} \times \frac{1}{2}$
7. $2\frac{5}{6} \times 1\frac{1}{4}$	**17.** Find $\frac{1}{2}$ of $2\frac{3}{4}$ ($\frac{1}{2} \times 2\frac{3}{4}$)
8. $1\frac{3}{4} \times \frac{2}{5}$	**18.** Find $\frac{3}{4}$ of $\frac{12}{17}$
9. $6\frac{2}{3} \times \frac{9}{10}$	**19.** Find $\frac{2}{3}$ of 14
10. $5\frac{3}{4} \times 1\frac{1}{5}$	**20.** Find $1\frac{1}{2} \times 3\frac{3}{4}$

9

Percentages—expressing one amount as a percentage of another

Sales, costs, profit or loss, discount, occupancy—all these are expressed in percentages and it is therefore very important to be able to understand and work out percentages.

Compare these two sets of figures showing profits for a three week period.

A. Week 1. $\frac{5}{36}$ of sales. Week 2. $\frac{4}{27}$ of sales. Week 3. $\frac{9}{80}$ of sales.
B. Week 1. 13.8% of sales. Week 2. 14.8% of sales. Week 3. 11.2% of sales.

It is much easier to compare line B to find that Week 2 had the best return on sales and yet lines A and B refer to the same weeks. It is usually more meaningful to express one amount as a percentage of another rather than as a fraction.

Example

a Express 3p as a % of 4p.

To find this comparison as a fraction, the 3p would be divided by the 4p to arrive at the answer $\frac{3}{4}$.

To express the answer as a % the fraction is multiplied by 100.

$$\frac{3}{4} \times \frac{100}{1} = 75\%$$

b Express £1.20 as a % of £4.00
(Always change to pence when any one amount contains pence.)

$$\frac{120}{400} \times \frac{100}{1} = 30\%$$

c What % of 44 is 32?

$$\frac{32}{44} \times \frac{100}{1} = 72.72\%$$

1. Express 32 as a % of 40.
2. Express 5p as a % of 25p
3. Express 40p as a % of 85p
4. Express £5.25 as a % of £10.00
5. Express 320 g as a % of 1 kg
6. Express 50p as a % of 78p
7. Express 4 kg as a % of 8.75 kg
8. Express 3 kg 125 g as a % of 5 kg
9. Express 12 litres as a % of 35 litres
10. Express £3500 as a % of £7750
11. What % of 55 is 45?
12. What % of £1.50 is £1.00?
13. What % of £0.15 is £0.04?
14. What % of 21 is 15?
15. What % of £1000 is £175?
16. What % of 15 kg is 3.125 kg?
17. What % of £8.00 is £3.20?
18. What % of 15 litres is 5 litres 200 ml?
19. What % of £42 is £28?
20. What % of £55.50 is £20.00?

10

Kitchen percentages

For purposes of control it is useful to be able to express the costs of various groups of items used in the kitchen (main course, vegetables, dairy, etc.,) as a percentage of either the total food and drink cost, or as a percentage of sales.

Example

Express each of the following costs as a percentage of the sales:

Meat £30.00
Vegetables £10.00
Sweet £7.50

Sales £120.00

Method

Meat $\frac{30}{120} \times \frac{100}{1} = 25\%$ of sales

Vegetables $\frac{10}{120} \times \frac{100}{1} = 8.33\%$ of sales

Sweet $\frac{750}{12\,000} \times \frac{100}{1} = 6.25\%$ of sales

Each group should remain fairly stable from period to period. A change in percentage should be thoroughly investigated and may be due to any of the following reasons:

a An increase in the cost of the item without a corresponding increase in the price charged.

b Poor portion control. An increase in the size of portions served would increase the percentage cost.

c Wastage through bad purchasing, poor preparation or incompetent cooking.

d Pilfering.

The increase in percentages caused by the above is due to an increase in costs needed to produce the same amount of sales. For instance, a meat cost of £100 required to produce sales of £500 would have risen to £150 if half of the meat had been wasted or stolen and the 20% meat to sales comparison would have risen to 30%.

1. Express each of the following costs as a percentage of the sales which were £175.00:

Soup £6.00, Meat £44.00, Vegetables £16.00, Sweets £16.00, Tea and Coffee £2.00.

2. The sales of a canteen for a week amounted to £1250. Give each of the following costs as a percentage of sales:

Vegetables £120, Meat £420, Dairy £200.

3. Give the following costs as a percentage of the total costs:

Meat £1000, Vegetables £240, Sweets £300, Drinks £150.

4. Express each cost as a percentage of the total costs:

   Dairy £250, Vegetables £120, Meat £500.

5. Express each of the following costs as a percentage of the £220.00 sales:

   Milk £12.00, Tea £25.20, Sugar £8.00.

6. A canteen sales were £3000. Express each of the following as a percentage of the sales:

   Meat £600, Vegetables £210, Sweets £160.

7. Give each of the following as a percentage of the receipts which were £2900:

   Meat £600, Vegetables £210, Sweets £160.

8. In one month the comparison of meat costs to sales was 17.5%. During the next month the statistics were as follows:

   Sales £5000, Vegetables £350, Meat £1100, Dairy £250, Coffee and Tea £150.

   Examine the two periods and give possible reasons for any difference.

11

Gross profit and costs

In the Hotel and Catering Industry gross profit is the difference between the price at which goods are sold and the price at which they were bought. It is sometimes referred to as 'Kitchen Profit'.

Example

The selling price of a dish is £1.20. The food cost of the dish is £0.44. Therefore the gross profit is 76p.

It is usual to express the gross profit as a percentage of the selling price.

Formula

$$\frac{\text{Gross Profit}}{\text{Selling Price}} \times \frac{100}{1}$$

e.g. $\frac{76}{120} \times \frac{100}{1} = \frac{190}{3} = 63.33\%$

Find the gross profit as a percentage of the selling price using the formula.

	Food cost	Selling price
1.	10p	40p
2.	£0.10	£0.15
3.	£25	£75
4.	3p	10p
5.	£1.25	£2.00
6.	£3	£5
7.	£0.70	£1.50
8.	£1	£2
9.	£3.50	£6.50
10.	£8.75	£25.00

11. The food cost of a dish is £0.35. Find the gross profit as a percentage of the selling price if the dish is sold for £0.80.

12. Goods are bought for £2.15 and sold for £3.50. Find the gross profit as a percentage of sales.

13. The ingredients cost of a cup of tea is $\frac{1}{2}$p. Find the gross profit as a percentage of sales if the tea is sold for 9p per cup.

14. The total sales in a canteen during a month were £1500.00 and the cost of all food and drink sold was £700. Find the gross profit as a percentage of sales.

15. A cake sold for 64p, cost 36p to produce. Calculate the profit as a percentage of the selling price.

16. A five course meal was priced at £5.75. If the food and beverage cost for this meal was £2.25, what was the gross profit as a percentage of the selling price?

17. The total cost of drinks sold at an hotel bar was £2460. If the takings amount to £5400, calculate the gross profit as a percentage of sales.

18. A catering manager aimed to make a gross profit of 65% on sales. During a week when food and drink costs amounted to £2050, the total sales were £5125. By how much did the actual gross profit percentage differ from the required percentage?

19. If a catering company made sales of £165 000 in a year and costs of food and drink were £65 000 find the profit and express it as a percentage of the sales.

20. If the food cost of a dish was 38% of its selling price, find the gross profit as a percentage of the selling price.

Sometimes we need to be aware of the Food or Drink *cost* percentage.

Example

The food cost of a dish is £0.30. The selling price of the dish is £1.05. Therefore the food cost as a percentage of sales is

$$\frac{30}{105} \times 100 = \frac{200}{7} = 28.57\%$$

1. The food cost of a dish is 25p. If the selling price of the dish is 70p, express the food cost as a percentage of the selling price.

2. The food cost of a dish priced at 75p is 25p.
a Express the food cost as a percentage of the selling price.
b Express the gross profit as a percentage of the selling price.

3. A cake was sold for £0.10. If the ingredient cost was £0.03, express this ingredient cost as a percentage of the selling price.

4. If the gross profit of a dish was 63% of the selling price, find the food cost as a percentage of the selling price.

5. A restaurant priced a bottle of wine at £2.75. If the cost of the wine to the restaurant was £1.50, express the cost as a percentage of the selling price.

12

Net profit

In finding the gross profit only the materials cost (food and drink) have been taken into account but there are two other costs that must be considered—labour and overheads.

Labour costs—include wages, staff meals, national insurance, staff accommodation and training.

Overheads include rates, rent, gas and electricity, telephone, stationery, insurance, advertising, repairs and depreciation.

Net profit is therefore the difference between the price at which goods are sold and the **total costs** (materials, labour, overheads).

These total costs are known as **The Elements of Costs**.

Example

The food cost of producing a dinner for The Evergreen Club was £37.50. The labour costs were reckoned at £23.25 and overheads estimated at £18.00. If The Evergreen Club was charged £93.75 for the dinner, calculate the net profit as a percentage of sales.

Food cost	£37.50	Sales	£93.75
Labour	£23.25	Total costs	£78.75
Overheads	£18.00	Net profit	£15.00
Total costs	£78.75		

The net profit (£15.00) is usually expressed as a percentage of sales.

$$\frac{1500}{9375} \times \frac{100}{1} = 16\%$$

1. Calculate the net profit as a percentage of sales from the following information:
   Food cost £3.20, Labour cost £3.00, Overheads £2.75, Sales £10.00.

2. The following figures were extracted from the books of The Blue

Moon Restaurant. Food cost £200.30, Labour and Overheads £295.00, Sales £550.00. Find as a percentage of sales **a** Gross profit **b** Net profit.

3. Find the percentage net profit on sales from the following statistics:
Food cost £80.00, Labour £75.00, Rent and Rates £30.00, Telephone £12.00, Stationery £8.00, Power £20.00, Sales £250.00.

4. A catering establishment made a gross profit of £1000. If labour costs were £450 and overheads £425 find the net profit.

5. If the gross profit was 60% of sales and the net profit was 10% of sales, calculate **a** the food cost as a percentage of sales **b** the total costs as a percentage of sales.

6. If the total cost to an hotel of a dinner for 50 guests was £195.00 and the guests were charged £4.50 per head, find **a** the net profit per cover **b** the net profit as a percentage of sales.

7. The returns for a school meals service were as follows:
Total receipts £10 000 Total costs £21 000
Calculate the net figure as a percentage of receipts.

8. **a** Is is possible for a function to show a gross profit but a net loss?
b Is it possible for a function to show a gross loss but a net profit?

9. A caterer quoted £300 as the price for a buffet at a wedding with 80 guests. If he allowed £1.25 per head for the cost of food and beverages, £75 for labour costs and £78 for overheads, calculate the net profit he expected as a percentage of the quote.

10. The total sales of a restaurant over a year amounted to £169 000. The cost of food and drink was £68 000 and Labour, Rent, Rates, Power and other costs totalled £85 000. What was the net profit as a percentage of the sales?

11. For a period of one week the returns of a catering establishment *A* were: Sales £12 500, Food cost £6000, Labour costs £3000, Overheads £2400.
Over the same period the returns for catering establishment *B* were: Sales £10 000, Food costs £3950, Labour costs £2550, Overheads £2500.
a Calculate
(i) the net profit of *A*
(ii) the net profit of *A* as a percentage of sales
(iii) the net profit of *B*
(iv) the net profit of *B* as a percentage of sales

b Which establishment do you think was the most successful? (For discussion.)

c If the owners of *A* and the owners of *B* had each invested £360 000 in their businesses which owner received the best percentage returns on his money?

d Should the net profit percentage of sales be the final consideration in assessing the success of a business? (Discussion.)

13

More about percentages

So far we have been concerned with expressing one amount as a percentage of another but it is also useful to be able to find a given percentage of an amount, e.g. find 3% of £25.50.

1% is one hundredth ($\frac{1}{100}$) and to find one hundredth of an amount we divide it by 100. There are two methods of working out this type of sum and both involve dividing by 100 to find 1% and then multiplying to find the required percentage.

Example

Find 3% of £25.50

Method 1

$$\frac{3 \times 25.50}{100} = \frac{76.50}{100} = £0.765$$

Method 2

1% of £25.50 = £0.255 (division by 100) therefore 3% = £0.765 (multiplication of decimals)

Find 1% of the following:

1. £570
2. £1425
3. £306
4. 455 kg
5. 25 litres
6. £126.50

7. Find 2% of £675
8. Find 6% of £1034
9. Find 20% of £2450
10. Find 8% of 175 kg
11. Find 15% of 250 litres
12. Find 4% of 500 kg
13. Find 35% of £4000
14. Find 2% of £5.75
15. Find 25% of £400
16. Find 10% of 140 kg
17. Find 20% of £25 000
18. Find 3% of £18.50
19. Find 5% of 75 kg
20. Find 40% of 80 litres
21. Find 16% of 5000 customers
22. Find 15% of 120 eggs

14

Percentage problems

1. 55% of hospital patients were on special diets. If on average there are 800 patients in a hospital calculate the number on diet.
2. An hotel manager required his chef to make a gross profit of 60% on sales. Calculate the gross profit the manager expected on sales of £1270.
3. A restaurant charged £4.75 + VAT for a meal. Find (i) the VAT

(ii) the total price charged (including VAT) if the rate of VAT was **a** 8% **b** 10% **c** 12%

4. A restaurant averaged 550 customers per week before raising prices which resulted in a drop of 4% of customers. How many customers are now served per week?

5. A caterer's sales amounted to £12 500. Find the overheads if the caterer estimated these to be 22% of sales.

6. A wine merchant advised all customers that prices would be increased by 6%. Find the new price of a bottle of wine previously sold for £3.60. (Give your answer to the nearest penny.)

7. A caterer allowed 12% for depreciation per year on the value of his large scale equipment. If he purchased a deep freeze for £225 find the estimated value after 12 months.

8. The electricity board announced a $2\frac{1}{2}$% increase in the price of electricity. If over the last 12 months an hotelier's electricity bill was £820, what could he expect to pay over the next 12 months assuming his electricity consumption stays constant.

9. A caterer always allowed 30% of sales as a charge to labour. Sales from a function brought in £1100 and he found that the labour cost was £305. Find the difference between his estimated labour cost and the actual labour cost.

10. The Inland Revenue allowed a caterer to reduce (depreciate) the value of his car by 25% per year for tax purposes. Calculate the value after one year of a car purchased for £3680.

11. If 55% was the percentage gross profit expected on the sales of drinks, calculate the estimated gross profit on drink-sales of £1270.

12. The food cost to an hotel for a period of a week was £800. If the hotelier estimated that the hotel staff meals accounted for 22% of the food cost what was the cost of the food consumed by the guests?

13. A chef reckoned that in frying fish there was an absorption of 12% of cooking oil. How much was remaining if the chef started with 5 litres of oil?

15

Discount

Giving discount, which means reducing the price of an article because the customer buys in bulk (Trade discount), or pays the bill promptly (Cash discount), is used much less now due to a number of factors. Price competition between suppliers means that prices differ without the action of discount. Shoppers will know how differing prices are asked for a jar of coffee. Drivers are aware of differences in the price of petrol. Customers can, and do, shop around to find the best price. The best price may not always be the lowest price when quality is considered. Many suppliers rely on huge volumes of trade to maintain their profitability, and in many cases profit margins are so low that giving discount can not be afforded.

Cash discount, which is offered for prompt payment, is almost non-existent now in the catering industry although a few suppliers may offer around 1% discount for quick payment. In certain industries (not food) it is *advantageous* for suppliers to sell on credit because finance houses (money lenders) give the suppliers a share of the interest charged to their customers.

Prices these days are often negotiable usually depending upon the amount of goods a customer purchases and are not likely to be quoted at a discount although it operates in a similar way to Trade discount.

Here are a few discount questions.

1. A restaurant owner buys goods amounting to £300 per month (at normal prices). Find the total money saved over 12 months if the rate of discount he received was 1%.

2. A dishwasher was priced by supplier A at £2056. The same model dishwasher was offered by supplier B at £2150 less 5% discount. Which supplier was the cheapest and by how much?

3. An advertisement by a supplier of cash registers read as follows, 'All manufacturers recommended prices slashed by 20%.' Find

the asking price for a cash register priced by the manufacturer at £425.00.

4. The central purchasing department of a Town Hall was given a 15% discount off all cleaning materials. Find the cost to the Schools' Meals Service of a drum of washing-up detergent if the usual advertised price was £18 per drum.

5. A firm offered $1\frac{1}{2}$% cash discount for prompt payment of bills and a customer could just afford to pay his bill but also needed money to buy extra equipment from another supplier. If the customer borrowed money from a bank he would be charged 12% interest. Do you think the customer would **a** pay the firm the money owed thereby receiving the cash discount and borrow the money required for the equipment from a bank?
OR
b not pay the firm, so losing the cash discount, and buy the equipment without having to borrow from the bank? (For discussion.)

16

Percentage puzzles

Example
a If 6p is 2% of an amount, what is 1%?

Method

6p = 2%

then $\frac{6}{2}$ = 1% (this is a very important mathematical step to understand)

therefore 3p = 1%

b If £24 is 8% of an amount, find 1%

If 24 $= 8\%$

then $\frac{24}{8} = 1\%$

$= £3$

1. If £50 = 25% find 1%
2. If £65 = 5% find 1%
3. If 36 kg = 24% find 1%
4. If 40 litres = 8% find 1%
5. If £250 = 16% find 1%

Example

c 6p is 2% of an amount, find 15%

Method

If 6p $= 2\%$

then $\frac{6}{2} = 1\%$

therefore $\frac{6}{2} \times \frac{15}{1} = 15\%$

$= 45$p

d If £0.70 = 20% find 32%

$\frac{70}{20} = 1\%$

$\frac{70}{20} \times \frac{32}{1} = 32\%$

$= £1.12$

e If 30 is 40% of a certain number, what is the number (100%)?

$\frac{30}{40} = 1\%$

$\frac{30}{40} \times \frac{100}{1} = 100\%$

$= 75$ (the number required)

6. If 21 is 35% of a number, what is the number?
7. If £0.14 is 20% of an amount, find 45%.
8. If 9 kg is 12% of an amount, find 80%.
9. If £33 is 11%, find 85%.
10. If 3 litres is 15%, find 100%.
11. If 81 kg is 18% of an amount find 20%.
12. 15% of a delivery of eggs were cracked. If 18 eggs were cracked, how many were delivered?
13. If 40% of the selling price of a dish was food cost, find the selling price if the food cost was £1.20.
14. If 15% was absorbed but 850 ml remained, calculate the original amount. (100%)
15. 16 girl students represented 80% of a class. How many students were in the class altogether?

17

Calculating the selling price

A bad pricing policy can quickly ruin a business. Overpricing will result in a loss of custom and under pricing can result in money being lost each time a dish is sold. A particular dish may be very popular because it is cheap (and underpriced) and so the more dishes sold the greater will be the loss.

One method of pricing a dish is to work on a fixed percentage of sales determined by experience.

A formula to remember:

$$\text{Cost} + \text{Profit} = \text{Selling Price } (100\%)$$

N.B. The selling price is always 100%

Example

a Find the selling price to achieve a gross profit of 60% on the selling price if the food cost is 36p.

Method

Cost + profit (60%) = selling price (100%)
therefore the cost = 40% (100% – 60%)
or 36p = 40%

$$\frac{36}{40} = 1\%$$

$$\frac{36}{40} \times \frac{100}{1} = 100\% \text{ (Selling price).}$$

$$= 90\text{p}$$

The selling price must be 90p.

b Find the sales necessary to achieve a net profit of 10% on sales if the total costs are £19.80.

Method

If the profit is 10% then the costs are 90%
therefore £19.80 (costs) = 90%

$$\frac{19.80}{90} \times \frac{100}{1} = 100\% \text{ (selling price)}$$

$$= £22.00$$

1. Find the selling price necessary to achieve a gross profit of 65% on the selling price if the food cost of a dish is £0.63.
2. A dish was costed out at 20p. What should be charged to achieve 60% gross profit on the selling price?
3. If the total costs for a buffet were £48.00, what should be charged to give a net profit of 12% on sales? (Answer to the nearest penny.)
4. The following figures were calculated for the Tigers Rugby

Club's annual dinner. Food cost £50, Labour and Overheads £85. What must be charged to achieve a net profit of 10% on sales?

5. The food cost of a dish was calculated as £1.35. What should be charged in order to make a 70% gross profit on the selling price?

6. In quoting for a luncheon a caterer estimated the costs as follows: Food £110, Labour £78, Overheads £83.
If the caterer allowed for a net profit of 10% on sales calculate the price quoted to the nearest £.

7. **a** Find the selling price of the following dishes in order to achieve a gross profit of $66\frac{2}{3}$% on the selling price.
Food costs (i) 25p (ii) 32p (iii) 42p

   b Compare the selling price with the food cost for each dish. Can you discover a simple method of finding the answer when the gross profit required is $66\frac{2}{3}$% of the selling price?

8. An hotelier wished to make 55% gross profit on sales for all drinks served at the bar. What must be charged for a bottle that cost the hotelier £1.80?

9. An industrial catering manageress was required to make 50% gross profit on sales. Find the charge made per meal if the average food cost of a meal was 35p.

10. The ingredient cost for a cup of tea was 1p. Calculate the charge per cup if 80% gross profit on the sales was made.

11. A chef was required to make 60% gross profit on sales. He had priced a dish at £2.40 but on costing the dish again he found the food cost had risen to £1.10. By how much should he increase the price to achieve the required gross profit?

12. Give the selling price to achieve a gross profit of $66\frac{2}{3}$% on sales if the ingredient cost was £1.95.

13. The total costs of a dinner for 100 guests were £380. What should be the charge per head in order to receive a net profit of 15% on sales? (Answer to nearest 10p.)

14. Discuss this statement, 'One fixed rate of percentage gross profit for every dish sold may not always be the best policy.' (Discussion.)

15. Find the selling price of a dish costing 95p to produce, if a gross

profit of 65% on the selling price was obtained. (Answer to nearest 5p.)

16. The total costs involved in catering for a disco were estimated at £140. If the caterer required a net profit of 10% on sales what should be charged to cater for this event? (Answer to nearest £.)

17. The £500 sales for a week showed a gross profit of 60% on sales. What should the sales have been in order to have made a gross profit of 65% on sales?

18. An industrial contract caterer required 12% net profit on sales. If the total costs per meal averaged £1.10, what subsidy per meal should be requested from the client if the price to the workers must be restricted to 60p per meal?

19. A canteen manageress aimed to make a gross profit of 60% on sales. The figures for the week were: Food cost £253.40, Sales £700.00.

a What was the actual gross profit achieved as a percentage of sales?

b By how much did the estimated gross profit differ from the actual gross profit?

20. What are the advantages and disadvantages of fixing selling prices *after* considering competitors prices? (For discussion.)

18

Wastage

Wastage occurs during preparation and cooking, it can be due to poor buying or lack of culinary skills. It is important to be able to calculate how much wastage occurs and to be able to order accordingly.

Example

A caterer took delivery of 20 kg of meat. After wastage in preparation and cooking only 14 kg of meat was served. What percentage of the original delivery was wasted?

Method

Delivery 20 kg
Served 14 kg

Wasted 6 kg
Percentage of delivery wasted

$$= \frac{6}{20} \times \frac{100}{1} = 30\%$$

1. Out of a delivery of 30 kg of meat there was a wastage of 12 kg. Calculate the percentage of the delivery that was wasted.

2. A caterer ordered and received 35 kg of meat. The meat produced eighty-four 125 g portions. What percentage of the original order was wasted?

Although it is useful to be able to find the percentage wasted, it is much more important to be able to calculate the correct amount to order *after* allowing for wastage.

Example

A caterer required to serve 14 kg of meat. By experience the caterer estimates that 30% of the meat would be wasted during the preparation and cooking. How much meat should the caterer order?

Method

Let amount of meat ordered = 100%
Amount wasted = 30% (of order)

Therefore meat to be served = 70% (of order)

But meat to be served = 14 kg
therefore 14 kg = 70% (of order)

therefore $100\% = \frac{14}{70} \times \frac{100}{1} = 20$ kg

Amount of meat to be ordered = 20 kg.

(Calculate all answers to nearest kg)

3. A chef estimated that he would require 13 kg of meat after wastage. If he allowed 35% for wastage, find the amount of meat the chef should order.

4. A caterer needed to serve 25 kg of meat. Calculate the amount of meat to be ordered if 40% was allowed for wastage.

5. Find the weight of fish to be ordered if a chef required 10 kg at the table and he estimated a wastage rate of 25% of delivery.

6. One hundred 120 g portions of meat were required. Allowing 45% for wastage, how much meat should be ordered?

7. A caterer required to serve 20 kg of meat. If he allowed 40% for wastage in preparation and cooking, calculate the total cost to the caterer if the meat was priced at £3 per kg.

8. Allowing 38% for wastage, calculate the amount of meat to be ordered if 35 kg was required to be served.

19

Bin cards

For the purposes of ordering and stock-taking it is important for a store keeper to be able to find out quickly and accurately how much of any item is in stock. There are various methods of doing this but the keeping of 'bin cards' is perhaps the most popular. The bin card can be attached to the shelf or bin where an item is stored and it is a simple matter for the storekeeper or manager to check the actual stock against the stock shown on the card.

The bin card shown below is a simple form although it is quite easy to add extra information such as 'minimum stock' to warn against running out of a certain item and 'maximum stock' to guard against stock deterioration.

BIN CARD No . . . . .

ITEM Flour   Unit . . . . 1.5 kg

DATE	RECEIVED	ISSUED	BALANCE
1st Mar	12	3	9
5th Mar		4	5
8th Mar	12	4	13

On March 8th the 12 bags received are added to the 5 bags balance on March 5th. After issuing 4 bags the final balance is 13 bags which should equal the number now in stock.

The final balance provides the necessary information to enable the storekeeper to decide whether to reorder and allows the manager to calculate the value of stock held. If flour was valued at £0.30 per kg then the value of the stock of flour on March 8th is £5.85.

Rule out bin cards for the following questions, enter the receipts and issues and find the balance in each case.

1. Sugar	April 4th	Received 20 kg	Issued 10 kg
	April 10th	Received 20 kg	Issued 5 kg
	April 15th		Issued 6 kg
2. Jam	Aug 3rd	Balance 14	
(5 kg tin)	Aug 6th	Received 6	Issued 2
	Aug 10th	Received 6	
3. Peaches	Oct 14th	Received 24	
(Tin)	Oct 15th		Issued 3
	Oct 18th	Received 12	Issued 4
4. Tea	June 1st	Received 14 kg	Issued 1 kg
	June 2nd		Issued 1 kg
	June 3rd		Issued 1.5 kg
	June 4th		Issued 0.5 kg
	June 5th		Issued 1 kg
	June 6th	Received 7 kg	Issued 1.75 kg
5. Margarine	Mar 3rd	Balance 14	
(250 g)	Mar 6th	Received 8	Issued 3
	Mar 8th		Issued 2
	Mar 10th		Issued 10
	Mar 12th	Received 8	
	Mar 13th		Issued 5
6. Eggs	Jan 4th	Received 120	
	Jan 5th		Issued 24
	Jan 6th		Issued 30
	Jan 7th		Issued 50
	Jan 8th	Received 120	Issued 10

20

Finding the cost of food and drink used—the cost of sales

The food cost of a single dish is usually found by reference to the costing sheet but to calculate the total food and drink cost of an establishment over a given period it is simpler to use the stock-take and purchases received.

Example

a The opening food stock on January 1st was £250 and the closing food stock on January 31st was £300. If the food purchases during January amounted to £700, calculate the cost of food used.

Method

Stock on January 1st	£250	Add to find
Purchases in January	£700	total available
	£950	
Stock on January 31st	£300	(subtract unused stock)
Cost of food used	£650	

b Food stock as at Jan 1st – £1 050
Food stock as at Dec 31st – £1 700
Food purchases during year – £10 000
Food purchases returns during year – £500
Calculate the cost of food used.

Method

Stock as at Jan 1st	£1 050	
Purchases less returns	9 500	(Add)
Total available	10 550	
Stock as at Dec 31st	1 700	(Subtract)
Cost of food used	£8 850	

In the examples above *Purchases* refer to all credit and cash purchases and *Purchases Returns* refer to any returns that have already been included under the heading of Purchases. When calculating the value of stock it is normal practice to take the lower of cost and market price. For example if a commodity was purchased at 10p per kg and the present price (market price) is 12p per kg then the value of the commodity is calculated at 10p per kg. If the cost price was 15p per kg and the market price is now 11p per kg the stock is calculated at 11p per kg.

1. Calculate the cost of food used from the following details: Opening stock £50, Closing stock £25, Purchases £40.
2. Find the cost of drink used from the following:
   Stock at 1st January £400, Stock at 31st January £450, Purchases during January £300.
3. Calculate the food cost from the following:
   Food stock as at 1st January £450, Food stock as at 31st December £700. Food purchases during the year £20 000, less food purchases returns £200.
4. Calculate the cost of sales from the following information:
   Opening stock on 1st March £75.50, stock at close of business on 31st March £120.25, purchases made during March £500.75.
5. The books of a small catering unit showed the following statistics for the month of June: Opening stock £90, Closing stock £100, Cash purchases £150, Credit purchases £350. Calculate the cost of the sales.
6. Find the cost of food used from the following:
   Stock as at 1st December £300, Stock as at 31st December £300, Local purchases in December £900, supplies from head office in December £150.
7. A business commenced operations on October 1st and during October food purchases amounting to £750 were made. If on October 31st the closing food stock was £85, find the cost of food used.
8. In question 7 what would be the opening stock on November 1st?
9. Calculate the cost of drinks used from the following information:
   Opening stock £908, Closing stock £700, Purchases £2000.
10. Find the cost of sales from the following details:
    Stock at 1st January £4000, Stock at 31st December £6000, Purchases during year £10 000.

11. Study the following information:
Food stock on 1st February £300, Stock on February 28th (according to the manager) £350, (according to the storekeeper) £370.
Purchases during February £645.
   a Find the food used (i) according to the manager (ii) according to the storekeeper.
   b Discuss why differences may occur (consider rising and falling prices).

21
The standard recipe

In a situation where a number of chefs are cooking in the same organisation it is usual to use the Standard Recipe. As its name suggests it is a method of standardising recipes so that there is a tight control on cost and quantity. Standardisation should not be allowed to stifle the individual chef's flair. It does mean that a Group Catering Manager can control quantities, quality and costs more easily.

The recipe lays down the ingredients, method of production and quantities used. It should give the number of portions to be served —this will determine the size of portion (portion control). A section giving variations can be added to reduce the total number of recipes required.

The advantages in using the standard recipe are:

a A well tried recipe ensures a consistently good finished product.
b It controls portion size which is so important in costing a dish.
c It is easy to determine the food cost of a particular dish.
d It simplifies the pricing of a particular dish.
e It reduces the possibility of error.

An example of a Standard Recipe form is shown below.

Recipe				No . . . .
Ingredients	Quantities		For	
	25	50	100	200
Method of Production			Comments	
Presentation for Service				
Variations	Variations of ingredients and method			

22

Costing sheets

Having decided on a particular dish it should be costed out accurately in order to fix the selling price and to find the profit.

A simple 'costing sheet' is set out below.

COSTING SHEET			
Dish	Date		
	Quantity	Unit cost	Total cost
Meat			
Poultry, Fish			
Greengrocery			
Dry Stores			
Total			
Number of portions			
Cost per portion			

Use the following prices in working out the questions.

Baking Powder	£0.35 per kg	Leeks	£0.48 per kg
Beef (Topside)	£3.25 per kg	Margarine	£0.65 per kg
Beer	£0.65 per litre	Milk	£0.27 per litre
Butter	£1.25 per kg	Onions	£0.20 per kg
Celery	£0.22 per kg	Onions (Button)	£0.45 per kg
Currants	£1.08 per kg	Potatoes	£0.09 per kg
Eggs	£0.60 per dozen	Suet	£0.72 per kg
Flour	£0.30 per kg	Sugar (Castor)	£0.40 per kg
Jam	£0.61 per kg	Sugar (Granulated)	£0.30 per kg
Lamb (stewing)	£1.20 per kg		

Draw costing sheets and find the cost *per portion* of the following. (Work to three decimal places of £.)

1. *Genoese Sponge*
(8 portions)

4 eggs
100 g castor sugar
100 g flour
50 g butter

2. *Shortbread Biscuits*
(12 portions)

150 g flour
50 g castor sugar
100 g margarine

3. *Steamed Currant Roll*
(6 portions)

300 g flour
15 g baking powder
75 g sugar
150 g chopped suet
100 g currants

4. *Queen of Puddings*
(4 portions)

500 ml milk
100 g castor sugar
25 g butter
50 g jam
3 eggs

5. *Carbonnade of beef*
(4 portions)

400 g lean beef (Topside)
15 g castor sugar
200 g sliced onion
250 ml beer

6. *Irish stew*
(4 portions)

425 g stewing lamb
400 g potatoes
100 g celery
100 g button onions
100 g onions
100 g leeks

23

Graphs

Graphs can be used effectively to display information in a simple, easy to read form. Comparing performance from lists of figures can be time-consuming and may lead to inaccuracies. A graph displayed on a wall can be a permanent reminder of the state of a catering enterprise.

Examine the line graph below.

The horizontal axis A–B refers to the months when a restaurant was in operation.

The vertical axis A–C refers to the sales made by the restaurant each month.

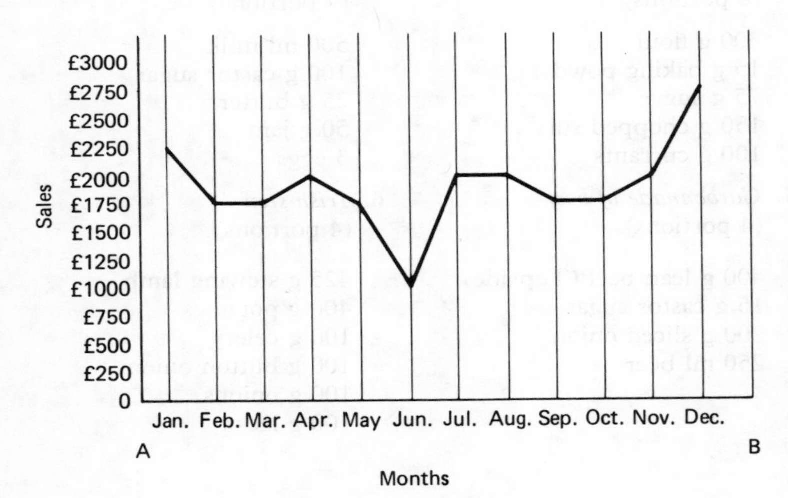

A Line graph

To determine the sales for March first find March on the horizontal axis and then find the plot vertically above. Read the sales figure £1750 in the left hand column level with the plot.

Answer the following questions by reference to the above graph.

1. What were the sales in July?
2. In which month do you consider the restaurant closed for 2 weeks?
3. What do you think was the reason for the December sales figure?

Here is an example of a block graph. This graph refers to the number of customers served in an industrial canteen during one week.

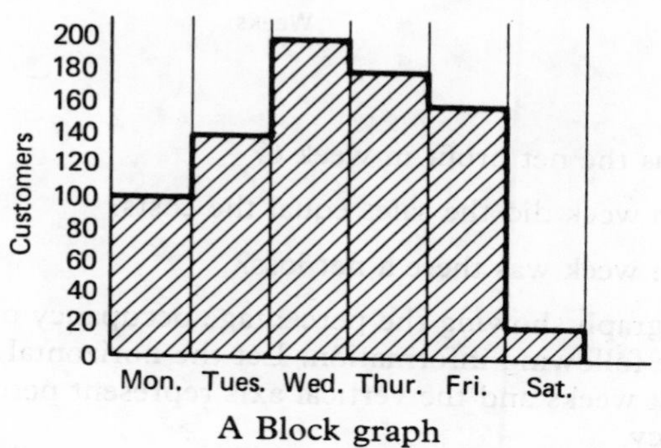

A Block graph

4. How many customers were served on Thursday?
5. Assuming the shape of the graph is typical of every week, on which day can the manageress reduce the staff to minimum cover?
6. On which two days must full staff cover be arranged?

More than one piece of information can be shown on a graph at one time. The graph over page shows two sets of facts. The continuous line shows the total sales for each week and the broken line shows the total costs. From these facts we can at a glance determine profit or loss.

The sales in week 1 were £1700 and the costs £1500, therefore the net profit was £200.

Notice how easy it is to detect any difference in the net profit from week to week.

7. In week 2.

   a What were the sales?
   b What were the total costs?
   c What was the net profit?

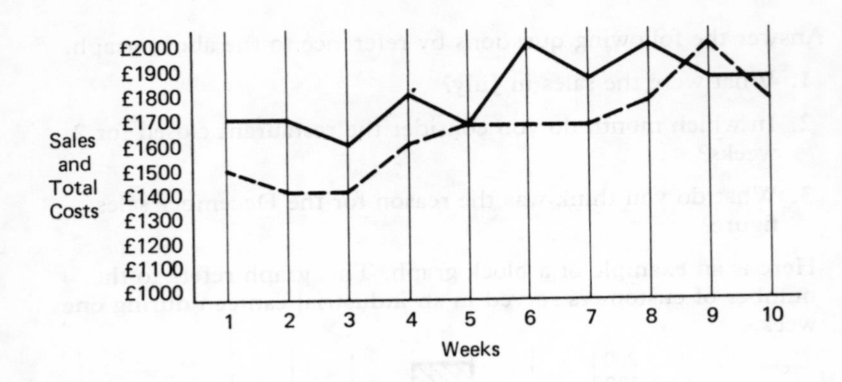

8. What was the net profit in week 6?

9. In which week did the sales equal the costs?

10. In which week was there a net loss?

11. Draw a graph showing the percentage occupancy of an hotel from the following information. Let the horizontal axis represent weeks and the vertical axis represent percentage occupancy.

Week 1. 40% occupancy. Week 2. 50% occupancy.
Week 3. 45% occupancy. Week 4. 60% occupancy.
Week 5. 75% occupancy.

12. Draw a graph to show the following information:

Month.	Jan	Feb	Mar	Apr	May	Jun	Jul	Aug	Sept	Oct	Nov	Dec
No. of customers.	400	300	250	300	300	350	300	250	350	350	400	500

13. Using ink to show customers and pencil to show sales, plot the following information on the same graph.

Day	Mon	Tues	Wed	Thurs	Fri	Sat
Customers	50	75	100	75	150	200
Sales	£100	£200	£225	£150	£500	£800

24

Pie charts

Another way of showing information is by the use of Pie Charts. Study the following diagrams.

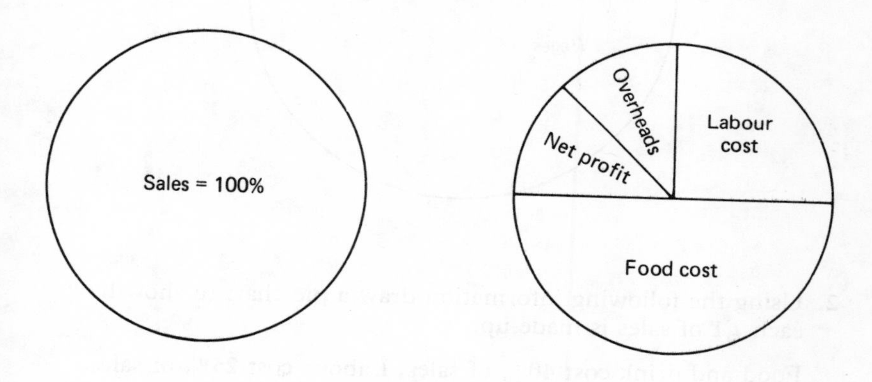

The circle (360°) is divided into segments according to the proportions of costs and profit of a Transport Cafe.

In the above example the area of the circle represents the total sales (100%)

The food cost of 50% of sales is represented by 50% of the area or 180° of the circumference (50% of 360°).

The labour cost of 25% of sales is represented by 25% of the area or 90° of the circumference (25% of 360°).

The overheads of 12.5% of sales are represented by 12.5% of the area or 45° of the circumference (12.5% of 360°).

The net profit of 12.5% of sales is similarly represented by 45°.

The chart can be enhanced by showing the various segments in different colours.

1. The following chart shows how the total labour costs of an hotel are divided. Measure the arc of each segment to find the value of each part of the total labour cost of £7200 per month.

N.B. First divide the £7200 by 360 to find the value of 1°.

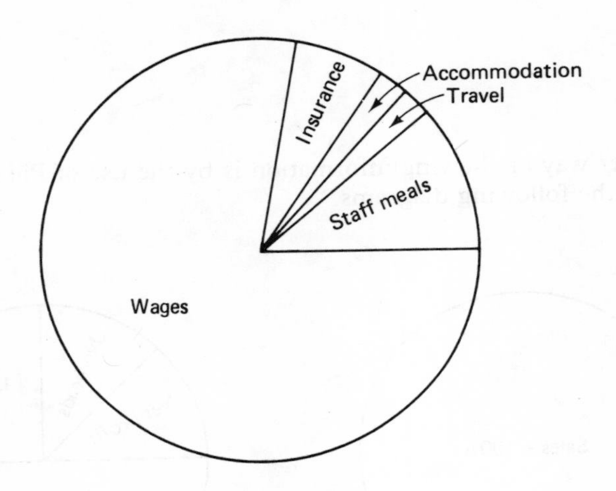

2. Using the following information draw a pie chart to show how each £1 of sales is made up.

Food and drink cost 40% of sales, Labour cost 25% of sales, Overheads 20% of sales, Net Profit 15% of sales.

3. The sales of an hotel in one week consisted of Accommodation £3600, Food £1200, Drink and Tobacco £600.
By means of a pie chart show these items as proportional parts of the total sales.

4. The total sales of a restaurant in one year are shown by the following pie chart. Find the value of each segment if the total sales represented were £180 000.

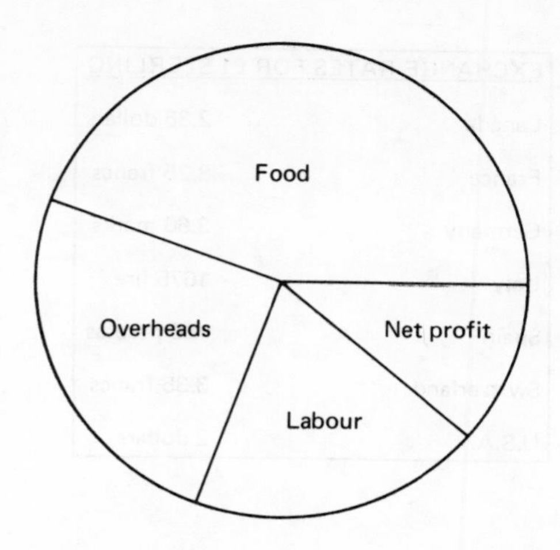

25

Currency conversion

The Hotel and Catering trade occupies a very important position in the tourist industry, earning a great deal of foreign currency for Great Britain. In this respect the Hotel and Catering trade acts as an *export trade* and greatly helps the *Balance of Trade*.

Foreign visitors mean foreign money and it is therefore sensible to be able to calculate the equivalent values of British and foreign money.

Study the following table.

EXCHANGE RATES FOR £1 STERLING	
Canada	2.36 dollars
France	8.25 francs
Germany	3.60 marks
Italy	1675 lire
Spain	150 pesetas
Switzerland	3.35 francs
U.S.A.	2 dollars

Examples using the above table:

a Calculate the sterling equivalent of 350 U.S.A. dollars.

$$\text{if 2 dollars} = £1$$
$$\text{then 350 dollars} = \frac{350}{2}\text{ pounds}$$
$$= £175$$

b How many U.S.A. dollars are equivalent to £90?

$$\text{if } £1 = 2\text{ dollars}$$
$$\text{then } £90 = 2 \times 90\text{ dollars}$$
$$= 180\text{ dollars}$$

c How many pounds sterling are equal in value to 300 French francs?

$$\text{if 8.25 fr} = £1$$
$$\text{then 300 fr} = \frac{300}{8.25}\text{ pounds}$$

Multiply top and bottom lines by 100

$$\frac{30\,000}{825}$$

Now cancel to make the sum simpler

$$\frac{1200}{33}$$
$$= £36.36$$

Work out the following using the exchange rates in the table provided:

1. How many pounds sterling are equivalent to 1000 U.S.A. dollars?
2. How many Spanish pesetas are equal in value to £25?
3. An hotel manager agreed to accept 500 French francs in payment of a bill for £50. Calculate the change given in pounds sterling.
4. Calculate the equivalent value of £50 in Italian lire.
5. A tourist wished to exchange £500 worth of travellers cheques for pesetas. Calculate how many pesetas he would receive.
6. An hotel cashed a travellers cheque for 100 Swiss francs. Calculate the amount of pounds sterling received by the tourist if the hotel deducted 2% commission.
7. How many Canadian dollars are equal to £200?
8. How many French francs should be obtained for £15?
9. How many pesetas should be requested from a potential Spanish tourist if an hotel required the equivalent of £20 deposit for a postal booking?

26

Twenty-four hour clock

An increase in the foreign tourist trade and closer links with the Continent mean there is an increasing use of the 24-hour clock system. Bus, train, boat and air timetables now use the 24-hour clock as this method helps to stop confusion over arrival and departure times.

Here are a few examples showing the same times for the 12 hour and 24 hour systems.

12 hour	*24 hour*
9 a.m.	09.00
10.30 a.m.	10.30
1.45 p.m.	13.45
8 p.m.	20.00

Notice that in the 24-hour system all times are calculated from mid-night and all times are represented by four figures (two figures for hours and two figures for minutes). Sometimes the word 'hours' is written after the figures, e.g. 14.25 hours.

Change the following to the 24-hour clock system:

1. 5 a.m. **2.** 12.25 p.m. **3.** 10 p.m. **4.** 2.10 a.m.
5. 11.27 a.m. **6.** Mid-day **7.** 11.55 p.m. **8.** 3 p.m.

Change the following to the 12 hour clock system:

9. 03.00 **10.** 17.30 **11.** 00.15 **12.** 16.00
13. 22.20 **14.** 11.28 **15.** 20.05 **16.** 13.00

Use the 24-hour clock in working out the following questions:

17. A dish which takes $2\frac{1}{2}$ hours to cook was placed in the oven at 16.35 hours. At what time will the dish be ready to serve?

18. At 10.40 hours an hotel receptionist took a phone message to say that a guest would be arriving in 4 hours time. At what time would the guest be expected to arrive?

19. A dish takes 3 hours 25 minutes to cook. At what time must the dish be placed in the oven in order to be ready to serve by 13.15 hours?

20. A guest requests a receptionist to find the time of arrival of a boat in Le Havre. The time table shows that the boat leaves Portsmouth at 10.20 hours and takes $5\frac{1}{2}$ hours to cross the channel. If the French authorities add 1 hour to British time (to conserve energy), at what time will the boat arrive in France?

21. Four dishes must be ready 15 minutes before the time of serving. Find the starting time for cooking each dish if they are to be served at 20.00 hours and they take the following cooking times:
Dish A $1\frac{1}{2}$ hours, Dish B 2 hours 10 minutes,
Dish C 45 minutes, Dish D 1 hour 20 minutes.

22. An hotel is to arrange for a guest to be met by car at an airport. If the flight leaves Germany at 23.04 and takes $1\frac{3}{4}$ hours at what time should the car be at the airport?

23. A telephone call was logged in to an hotel at 2 minutes past mid-night. Write this time according to the 24-hour clock.

Mixed tests

Test 1

1. Find the total week's taking of a cafe if the daily receipts were:
   Monday £150.12, Tuesday £148.08,
   Wednesday £250.90, Thursday £47.03,
   Friday £184.75, Saturday £215.15
2. If question one referred to a week when cost of food and drink was £328.34 calculate the gross profit.
3. The average weekly wage bill for an industrial canteen was £308.32. Calculate the total wages paid in one year.
4. The total ingredient cost for 25 covers was £15.85. Find the cost per cover to the nearest penny.
5. **a** Find 40% of £300.
   b Allowing 35% wastage in preparation and cooking, calculate weight of meat remaining to be served from a delivery of 40 kg.
6. Find the cost of buying 50 kg of sugar at £0.28 per kg.
7. During one week the sales amounted to £347.57. What was the net profit if the food cost was £120.50, the labour cost was £95.72 and the overheads cost was £92.05?
8. Cancel **a** $\frac{34}{51}$ **b** $\frac{14}{84}$ **c** $\frac{150}{1000}$
9. **a** $\frac{3}{7} \times \frac{2}{3}$ **b** $\frac{2}{3} \times \frac{9}{11}$ **c** $4\frac{1}{6} \times \frac{3}{5}$
10. Find the cost of 600 ml if 1 litre costs 25p.

Test 2

1. Total the following bill.

   4 kg at £0.09½ per kg
   1.5 kg at £0.32 per kg
   4.125 litres at £0.80 per litre
   150 g at £1.00 per kg

2. Find the food cost for March from the following figures:

Opening food stock as at 1st March	£205
Closing food stock as at 31st March	£293
Food purchases during March	£348

3. If the food cost is £78 and the sales are £210 calculate the gross profit.

4. Find the total receipts if the following amounts of money were taken during one day:

   4 × £10, 7 × £5, 14 × £1, 23 × 50p, 20 × 10p, 18 × 5p, 45 × 2p, 52 × 1p, 17 × $\frac{1}{2}$p.

5. Find the cost of buying 3 kg if 25 g cost £0.04.

6. If the total sales were £550 express each of the following as a percentage of sales:

   Meat £60, Vegetables £38, Sweets £40, Tea and Coffee £7.

7. Express 4372 g in kilogrammes.

8. An analysis of the cash register showed that 1200 customers spent £1350. How much did the average customer spend?

9. If £32 represents 12% of an amount, find 39%.

10. From 2 litres of cooking oil, 175 ml was absorbed. What percentage of the original amount was absorbed?

Test 3

1. The following details were taken from the books of The Stag Hotel:
   Food cost £305.00, Labour cost £275.00, Overheads cost £225.00, Sales £900.00.
   Calculate **a** The gross profit as a percentage of sales.
   b The net profit as a percentage of sales.

2. One hundred 125 g portions of meat are required to be served. Allowing 40% for wastage, calculate how many kg of meat should be ordered (to nearest kg).

3. The original price of goods bought by a caterer was £83.50. He was allowed a trade discount of 20%. Calculate the amount paid by the caterer.

4. Find $17\frac{1}{2}\%$ of £350.

5. If the food cost of a dish was £0.34 calculate the price that should be charged for this dish in order to achieve a profit of 65% on the selling price.

6. A dish was priced at £1.05 and the food cost of the dish was £0.35. Find the gross profit as a percentage of the selling price.

7. Find the cost of sales during June from the following details:

Stock at 1st June £205.00, Stock at 30th June £180.00, Credit purchases £508.00, Cash purchases £28.00, Purchases Returns £15.00.

8. An hotel has 65 bedrooms. If 26 bedrooms are not occupied, what is the percentage occupancy?

9. The food and beverages cost of an industrial canteen during one 5 day week was £800. If daily receipts from sales were £130 calculate the subsidy per meal if on average 200 meals were served.

10. **a** Find the sales from 10 000 cups of coffee sold at £0.20 per cup.
b If the sales from 2000 meals totalled £4100 find the average charge per meal.

Test 4

1. The following are the costs of a dish to produce 20 portions.

4 kg at £0.45 per kg
2.5 kg at £0.66 per kg
200 g at £0.75 per kg

a Calculate the cost per cover.
b (i) Find the selling price per cover to achieve a profit of 60% on the selling price.
(ii) Find the gross profit per cover.
c Find the profit as a percentage of the selling price if the selling price was £0.50 per cover.

2. The following statistics were taken from the book of The Sea View Hotel:

	£
Stock at 1st February	£316
Stock at 28th February	£350
Purchases during February	£410
Sales	£1000

a Find the cost of sales. (Food and Drink cost.)
b Calculate the gross profit as a percentage of sales.

3. For a dinner for 100 guests the charge per head is £4.45. Gross profit is 55% of sales. Labour cost is £105.75. Overhead cost is £95.00.
Find a The food cost for 100 covers.
b The net profit per cover.

4. The manager of a works canteen covers all expenses when charging for the 200 meals he produces each day for 5 days a week.

If food costs amount to £400 per week and labour and overheads amount to £250 per week, calculate the average selling price per meal.

5. A canteen assistant earns £1.20 per hour. Calculate her gross wage in a 5 day week if she works from 9 a.m. until 4.30 p.m., with a break of 1 hour for lunch.

6. Find the cost of 75 g if 1 kilogram costs £1.60.

Test 5

1. Draw a graph to represent the following information:

Sales	£8500	£8000	£8600	£8600	£8500	£8900	£9000	£8900	£8800	£8900	£9000	£9000
Months	Jan	Feb	Mar	Apr	May	Jun	July	Aug	Sept	Oct	Nov	Dec

2. The following statistics were extracted from the books of a catering establishment during February:
Meat cost £1232, Vegetables cost £740, Dry goods cost £836, Beverages cost £292, Sales £8000.

a Express each cost as a percentage of the sales.
b A check in March revealed the Meat cost to be 20% of sales. Give possible reasons for this increase.

3. a Find the cost of 5.125 kg at £0.12 per kg.
b Find the cost of 375 g at £3.00 per kg.

4. a Change to mixed numbers (i) $\frac{23}{8}$ (ii) $\frac{52}{17}$.
b Change to improper fractions (i) $3\frac{2}{7}$ (ii) $11\frac{3}{5}$.

5. A caterer ordered and received 50 kg of meat costing £2.50 per kg.
a If 37.5% was wasted in preparation and cooking, how many portions each of 125 g can be produced?
b Calculate the cost per portion to the caterer.

6. The following figures were taken from the books of The Chestnut Restaurant during the month of July:

	£
Food Cost	2400
Full-time labour costs	1620
Part-time labour costs	300
Rates	630
Power	525
Renewals	144
Advertising	105
Telephone	75
Stationery	45
Sales	7200

Find as a percentage of sales:
a the gross profit
b the net profit
c the labour costs
d the total costs.

Test 6

1. The total food cost of a dinner for 40 guests was £60.86. If the labour cost is reckoned at £38.05 and the overheads estimated at 25% of sales, calculate the charge per cover to give a net profit of 12% on sales (Answer to nearest 10p).

2. One hundred and twelve 125 g portions of meat are required to be served **a** If 30% is allowed for wastage find how many kg of meat must be ordered.
b If the cost price of the meat is £2.80 per kg find the gross profit as a percentage of the selling price assuming each portion is sold for £1.50.

3. The price of a stores order was £35.05. If the discount allowed was 15% calculate the amount paid.

4. Write the following amounts to the nearest penny:
a £14.0148 **b** £25.17841 **c** £0.84½.

5. From a delivery of 275 kg of potatoes, 15.5 kg were found to be unusable. What percentage of the delivery could be used?

6. The total takings of a cafe during one week were as follows:
Monday £75.60 Tuesday £83.05 Wednesday £104.00
Thursday £80.75 Friday £125.44 Saturday £208.15

a Calculate the gross profit as a percentage of sales if the food and drink costs were £244.00 and the VAT payable on the sales was £51.99.
b During the week there were 770 customers. How much did the average customer spend? (to nearest penny)
c In the next week there was a 20% increase in customers and the average customer spent £0.95. Find the total takings for the week.

Test 7

1. Write the following amounts corrected to 2 decimal places of £1.
   a £0.1782   b £14.205   c £0.87477

2. Draw a bin card, enter the following details and show the balance at the end of the week:

Item. Jam	Unit. kg	
3rd July	Balance 10	
4th July	Received 5	Issued 3
5th July		Issued 2
6th July	Received 10	
7th July		Issued 6
8th July	Received 5	Issued 3

3. The following figures were taken from the books of The Elizabethan Restaurant:

	£
Food stock at 1st January	610
Food stock at 31st January	804
Cash purchases during January	90
Credit purchases during January	1700
Purchase Returns during January	30
Sales during January	4000

   a Calculate (i) the food cost during January (ii) the gross profit during January.
   b What was the opening food stock at 1st February?

4. The following ingredients are required to produce 4 portions of chicken and bacon pie:

   1.25 kg Chickens at £1.10 per kg
   225 g flour (bread) at £0.35 per kg
   125 g pastry margarine at £0.64 per kg
   25 g cake margarine at £0.60 per kg
   100 g bacon at £1.80 per kg
   1 egg at £0.60 per dozen

50 g chopped onions at £1.50 kg
25 g onions at £0.20 per kg
Sundries—estimated cost £0.05.

a Find the cost per portion (to nearest penny).
b Find the selling price per portion to achieve a profit of 60% on the selling price (to nearest penny).
c If the selling price per portion was £1.50 what was the profit as a percentage of the selling price?

5. Express **a** 3 kg 25 g in grammes **b** 7148 g in kg
c 4.25 litres in ml **d** 6 litres 35 ml in litres.

6. Explain the importance of each of the following:

a Good buying **b** Careful preparation and cooking
c Portion control **d** Correct selling price.

Test 8

1. a What are 'The Elements of Cost'?
b Under which Element of Cost would you place:
(i) Gas (ii) Staff meals (iii) Meat (iv) Depreciation
(v) Telephone.

2. A cook requires 17 kg of meat on the plates. Allowing 32% for wastage **a** how much meat should be ordered? **b** What will be the cost at £3.25 per kg?

3. An hotel had 20 double-bedrooms at £10.50 per person and 30 single-bedrooms at £12.25 per person. 13 double bedrooms and 18 single bedrooms were fully occupied.
a Find the percentage occupancy of (i) the double-bedrooms (ii) the single-bedrooms (iii) the hotel as a whole.
b If the total sales for the day were £900, calculate the receipts from the apartments as a percentage of the total sales.

4. The following figures were taken from the books of The Sea View Restaurant for the month of April:

	£
Food cost	3900
Full time labour	2460
Part time labour	300
Rent Rates	1320
Telephone	180
Gas and Electricity	936
Insurance	168
Depreciation and Renewals	192
Advertising	138
Sales	11 700

Find **a** the gross profit as a percentage of sales
b the net profit as a percentage of sales
c the overheads as a percentage of sales.

5. If £2.50 was required as the returns for a dish in order to give a 60% profit on sales before the addition of VAT, calculate the price a customer must pay if the rate of VAT was:
a 8% **b** 10% **c** 12%.

6. A domestic assistant's hours of work were as follows: Monday 9 a.m.–6 p.m., Tuesday 8.30 a.m.–5 p.m., Wednesday 8.30 a.m.–5.30 p.m., Thursday 9 a.m.–6 p.m., Friday 8.30 a.m.–5 p.m. Calculate her wages per week if the hourly rate of pay was £1.25 for the first 37 hours worked and £1.65 per hour for any hours worked in excess of 37. (Allow 1 hour per day for lunch.)

Test 9

1. During one week a caterer make £555 gross profit, which was 60% of sales. Labour costs were £225 and overheads £240.
a Find (i) the sales (ii) the net profit (iii) the net profit as a percentage of sales.
b If the labour costs had been £280 and the overheads £290, what is the term given to the net figure?

2. At the end of a six month period it was found that food costs had increased by 5% and yet the gross profit percentage had remained at 65% of sales. How was this possible if the following assumptions are made?
(i) There was no decrease in wastage.
(ii) Portion size had remained constant.
(iii) There had never been any pilfering.

3. The stock records of a catering establishment showed the following details for the month of February:

Opening food stock on February 1st	£705
Food Purchases	£510

The closing food stock was valued at £800 by the storekeeper but at £775 by the manager.
The sales during February were £1300.
a Calculate the food cost in February (i) according to the storekeeper (ii) according to the manager.
b Calculate the gross profit as a percentage of sales (i) according to the storekeeper (ii) according tot he manager.
c Give possible reasons for this difference and discuss the

fairness of valuing stock at the lower of cost or market price in times of inflation.

4. A school meals service produces 10 000 meals each day on 5 days per week for 40 weeks in a year. The total food costs are £700 000, labour and overheads amount to £750 000 per year.
   a Calculate the food cost per meal.
   b If the charge per meal is 30p, find the subsidy paid on each meal.

5. From the information shown in the table below plot the two sets of information on one graph.

Day	Mon	Tues	Wed	Thurs	Fri	Sat
Customers	50	60	60	45	75	95
Sales	£115	£120	£150	£80	£225	£285

6. Write down the advantages to a catering group of introducing the 'standard recipe'.

Test 10

1. **a** A caterer was asked to plan a dinner for 50 guests each paying £5.25. The labour costs were estimated to be: full-time £45.00 and part-time £20.00. Overheads are reckoned as 20% of sales.
   Calculate how much can be spent on food per cover if a net profit of 10% on sales is required.
   b New food prices show there is an increase of 10p per cover. The management decide to keep the same menu and not to increase the charge for the dinner. Calculate the net profit percentage of sales using the new prices.

2. The following ingredients are required to produce 8 portions of Braised Liver and Onions.

   700 g ox liver at £0.90 per kg
   100 g lard at £0.50 per kg
   100 g flour at £0.30 per kg
   450 g onions at £0.20 per kg
   1 litre of stock, estimated cost £0.14 per litre.

   a Calculate
   (i) the total food costs.
   (ii) the cost per portion (to nearest penny).
   (iii) the profit as a percentage of the selling price if the portions are sold at 40p each.
   b Does question (iii) above refer to Gross or Net profit?

3. The following figures were taken from the books of The Blue Bell Restaurant referring to the month of August.

Stock at 1st August	£528.00
Stock at 31st August	£384.00
Purchases during August	£591.00
Purchases returns in August	£12.80
Labour cost—Full time	£463.40
Part time	£102.40
Rent and Rates	£166.00
Depreciation	£61.00
Postage and Stationery	£32.28
Telephone	£72.92
Insurance	£52.00
Gas and Electricity	£97.20
Advertising	£45.28
Sales	£2100.00

a Find the gross profit as a percentage of sales.
b the net profit as a percentage of sales.
c the labour cost as a percentage of sales.
d the total costs as a percentage of sales. (Try and work this out by studying the answer to **b**.)

4. The daily occupancy of an hotel capable of sleeping 50 guests was as follows:

Monday 20	Tuesday 36	Wednesday 28	Thursday 25
Friday 35	Saturday 48	Sunday 15	

What was the percentage occupancy for the week?

Test 11

1. An industrial canteen manager aimed to make a gross profit of 55% on sales. The figures for the first month showed that out of sales of £5000 the gross profit was 48% on sales.
a By how much money did the 'actual' sales differ from the 'aimed for' sales? (to the nearest £.).
b On closer examination it was found that the food costs included the cost of staff meals which amounted to £400. Give the corrected gross profit as a percentage of the sales.

2. The organisers of a garden fete sold 500 cups of tea at 8p each. The costs were as follows:
Tea: 1 kg at £0.64 kg
Milk: 2 litres at £0.27 litre
Sugar: 1.75 kg at £0.30 kg

a Find the gross profit.
b Find the gross profit as a percentage of sales.
c At a similar fete a month later it was decided to raise the price of the tea to 9p per cup. This resulted in the number of cups sold being reduced by one quarter and similarly the total ingredient cost was reduced by a quarter.
(i) Find the new gross profit at the second fete.
(ii) Express the gross profit as a percentage of sales.
(iii) Say with reasons, which was a better price from a money-raising point of view (Discussion).

3. A caterer required to serve two hundred 125 g portions of meat. If he bought from supplier A at £2.70 per kg, an allowance of 40% should be made for wastage. If he bought from supplier B at £3.10 per kg, an allowance of 35% should be made for wastage.
a If supplier A was selected, how many kg of meat should be ordered? (Answer to nearest kg)
b If supplier B was selected, how many kg of meat should be ordered? (Answer to nearest kg)
c Which is the best buy (on the information given).
d Discuss other factors that should be taken into account.

4. R. Bryon commenced business on January 1st. The following details relate to his food Purchases and Sales in the first two months.

	£	
Jan 10 Purchases	300	Sales during January £725
Jan 31 Closing Stock	50	
Feb 5 Purchases	200	Sales during February £1050
Feb 23 Purchases	150	
Feb 28 Closing Stock	75	

a Calculate the cost of food in (i) January (ii) February.
b Calculate the gross profit in (i) January (ii) February.

Test 12

1. A catering manager aimed to make a gross profit of 65% on sales. The £450 food sales for one week showed a gross profit of 60% on sales and a net profit of 10% on sales.
a What was the actual food cost?
b What should the sales have been in order to have achieved the aim of the manager? (To nearest £.)
c If the labour cost was £125 express the overhead cost as a percentage of the actual sales.

2. The following ingredients are required to produce 8 portions of Spaghetti Bolognaise:

Spaghetti	250 g at £0.60 per kg
Parmesan Cheese	100 g at £0.12 per 25 kg
Stewing Beef	200 g at £1.95 per kg
Chopped Onions	100 g at £0.20 per kg
Butter	25 g at £1.20 per kg
Garlic	10 g at a cost of £0.02
Jus lie	250 ml estimated cost £0.10

a Find the total ingredient cost *per portion* (to nearest penny).
b Find the selling price per portion to achieve a 60% profit on sales.
c If the selling price was £0.50 per portion, express the profit as a percentage of sales.

3. The following statistics were taken from the books of The Waterside Hotel:

	£
Food Stock at 1st Feb.	820
Food Stock at 28th Feb.	1068
Food Purchases during Feb.	1684
Food Purchases Returns in Feb.	16
Labour cost	1100
Rent and Rates	480
Telephone	50
Power	276
Stationery	36
Advertising	50
Depreciation and Renewals	40
Insurance	76
Sales	4200

Find **a** Food cost **b** Gross profit as a percentage of sales.
c Net profit as a percentage of sales.

4. You have been asked to plan a dinner for 50 guests paying £6.00 per head. The labour cost is estimated to be: full time £60.00; part-time £15.00. Overheads are reckoned as 20% of sales. Calculate how much can be spent on food per cover if a net profit of 10% on sales is required.

Test 13

1. The following costs and sales refer to two differing types of

catering establishments. One is a high-class restaurant and the other a self-service cafeteria.

	A £	*B* £
Food	1050	700
Labour	870	480
Overheads	896	492
Sales	3200	1900

a Calculate as a percentage of sales for each establishment:
(i) Gross profit (ii) labour cost
(iii) overheads (iv) net profit

b Say with reasons which you consider to be the High-Class restaurant.

2. How can an increase in sales increase the net profit as a percentage of sales without necessarily increasing the gross profit as a percentage of sales? (Discussion.)

3. A chef served forty-eight 125 g portions of meat and charged £1.25 per portion. The meat cost the chef £2.50 per kg and an allowance of 40% was made for wastage.
Find **a** the total cost of the meat to the chef.
b the gross profit as a percentage of the selling price.

4. The Falcon Hotel has 75 double-rooms and 50 single-rooms. The charge for a double-room is £16 and for a single-room £9. The guests' tabular ledger showed the following rooms fully occupied.

	Mon	Tues	Wed	Thurs	Fri	Sat	Sun
Double rooms	40	40	30	35	50	60	45
Single rooms	30	40	50	50	50	25	25

Calculate: **a** the total receipts from rooms for the week.
b the actual guest occupancy as a percentage of the possible guest occupancy.
c plot both sets of figures (double and single rooms) on the same graph.

Test 14

1. The Bursar of a college hall of residence hoped to cover all expenses during a year of 52 weeks. The normal college year was of 30 weeks duration. Income from students amounted to £400 per week during term time. Expenses were as follows:

Food and Beverages—£220 per week during term time.
Labour and Overheads—£150 per week for the full 52 weeks.

There was a chance of three conferences of equal length being held at the hall during vacations, accommodating 30, 45 and 40 persons respectively. The cost of food and beverages for these conferences would be £20 per head.

a Calculate to the nearest £1 the quote per person that the Bursar should give to the conference organisers in order to cover all expenses for the year.
b The conference organiser replies that he will only take the hall at £35 per person. Should the Bursar accept this offer if there is no possibility of other bookings? (Give figures to support your answer.)
c If the Bursar accepted the terms, calculate the expected costs to be covered for the year as a percentage of the total costs.

2. The books of a catering company showed the following facts:

	£
Food stock at 1st June	506
Food stock at 30th June	610
Food purchases in June	740
Food purchases returns	25
Sales in June	1530

The expected gross profit was 65% of sales.
Calculate: **a** the food cost during June.
b the actual gross profit as a percentage of sales.
c the difference between the actual and expected gross profit. (To the nearest £.)

3. A caterer required the following profit on his receipts: on dish A—60% on dish B—50% on dish C—65%.
The food costs of the dishes are: A—£0.70, B—£1.25, C—£1.75.
Allowing for VAT rate of 10%, what must be the charge for each dish? (Answers to nearest penny.)

4. Consider the question and answer to **1b** in discussing the following: 'Is it advantageous under certain circumstances to sell a dish that will give a net loss but a gross profit?'

Examination papers

EAST MIDLANDS EDUCATIONAL
UNION EXAMINATION 1973
FOOD COSTING I

ATTEMPT FIVE QUESTIONS—
TIME ALLOWED 1½ HOURS

1. a (i) A catering establishment purchases milk in 3 gallon containers at £0.45 per gallon. This establishment uses 25 pints per day and opens for 6 days a week. Calculate the cost of milk during a 4-week period. (No milk is wasted.)

(ii) If the establishment sold third-pint glasses of milk for 3p each, calculate the profit on 1 gallon of milk.

b In one week the food cost of a canteen in producing 1150 meals was £240.00. Find the average food cost per meal.

c (i) Find the cost of making 1000 cakes at £0.01 each.

(ii) 100 cups of coffee were sold for £5.50. Find the charge per cup.

2. a The terms of a supplier of goods were as follows:

Trade discount: 15%
Cash discount: 8% if paid within 14 days of receipt of invoice;
3% if paid within 28 days of receipt of invoice.

A caterer ordered and received goods to the value of £57.60 and received the invoice on February 20th 1973. Calculate the price he would pay if he sent off his cheque in payment of the goods on March 12th 1973.

b Why do suppliers allow cash discount?

3. The following figures were extracted from the books of the Hillside Restaurant for the month of April:

	£
Food cost	650
Full-time labour costs	410
Part-time labour costs	50
Rent and Rates	220
Telephone	30
Gas and Electricity	156
Insurance	28
Depreciation and Renewals	32
Advertising	23
Sales	1950

Find:

a the gross profit as a percentage of sales,
b the net profit as a percentage of sales,
c the labour cost as a percentage of sales,
d the total costs as a percentage of sales.

4. Assume 1.8 pints is equal to 1 litre and 2.2 lb is equal to 1 kg.

a (i) How many kilograms are equal to 1 cwt?
(ii) How many litres are equal to 5 gallons?
(iii) Find the cost per litre if 1 pint costs £0.05.
(iv) What is the difference in price per lb of the following:
Old price $4\frac{1}{2}$p per lb.
New price 11p per kilogram?

b Express 4 kg 350 g in kilograms.

5. **a** What are the objects and advantages of food-costing?
b Write brief notes on the documents used in food-costing.

6. A caterer required the following profit on the selling price: On dish A 60%; on dish B 45% and on coffee 80%.

a Find the selling price of each of the above if the costs were: (i) dish A £0.25; (ii) dish B £0.88; (iii) coffee £0.01½.
b List the factors that must be considered when deciding on the selling price.
c How will Value Added Tax affect the selling price of a meal in a restaurant? If the price of a meal before the addition of VAT was £1.00, give an example (showing the percentage VAT) to indicate the price the customer might have to pay.

7. The food costs of a canteen for October were:

meat £500; vegetables £305; sweets £325.

The sales receipts during October were £1900.

a Express each cost as a percentage of sales.
b During November the cost for meat was £600 and the sales increased to £2000.

(i) Find the new percentage of meat cost to sales.
(ii) Give possible reasons for the differences between the two months.

8. The opening stock at the beginning of August of a catering establishment was £500.
Credit purchases during August amounted to £600.
Cash purchases during August amounted to £50.
At the end of August the storekeeper estimated the closing stock to be £300.
The manager estimated the closing stock to be £325.
The sales during August were £2500.

a Calculate the cost of sales (food used) during (i) the storekeeper's figure and (ii) the manager's figure.
b What is the difference in the percentage profit on sales when comparing the two answers to part **a**?
c Prices were rising during this period and either the manager or the storekeeper took the latest market price of the goods in stock.

(i) Which person took the latest market price of the stock?
(ii) Is this usual trade practice?

EAST MIDLANDS EDUCATIONAL UNION EXAMINATION 1975 FOOD COSTING I

ATTEMPT FIVE QUESTIONS— TIME ALLOWED 1½ HOURS

1. a On average an employee paid the following amounts for one week for each of his twelve staff:

Gross wages £22.50, National Insurance £1.72, Transport £0.74, Estimated cost of meals £1.20.

(i) Find the total labour cost for a fifty week year (ignore holiday costs).
(ii) What percentage of the total labour cost are the gross wages?

b During April the total takings of a restaurant were £4800 (including VAT). In that month 5000 customers were served.

(i) Find the average amount spent by each customer.
(ii) Calculate the amount of gross profit if the VAT on these sales was £350 and the restaurant made a gross profit of 65% on sales.

c Express:

(i) 1 kilogram in pounds,
(ii) 1 litre in pints.

2. The following is an extract taken from an invoice sent to a caterer:

1 gross at £0.25 per dozen
5 litres at £0.085 per litre
4.5 kg at £0.35 per 250 grams
20 bottles at £1.05 each

The suppliers terms were as follows:

Trade discount:	15%
Cash discount:	4%

a Calculate:

(i) the total bill before any discount,
(ii) the total amount to be sent by the caterer to the supplier if the caterer received both trade and cash discount.

b List the checks that should be made before an invoice is passed for payment.

3. a A catering establishment commenced on 1st April, 1975. During April food purchases amounted to £400 and sales £800 (exclusive of VAT). Food stock held on 30th April was £100. Calculate:

(i) the cost of sales (food cost) for April,
(ii) the gross profit as a percentage of sales for April.

b During May food purchases amounted to £500 and sales £1200 (exclusive of VAT). Food stock held on 31st May was £200. Calculate:

(i) the cost of sales for May,
(ii) the gross profit as a percentage of sales for May.

c Which of the following should be taken into account when calculating the gross profit in a catering establishment:

(i) stationery, (ii) potatoes, (iii) petrol for owner's car, (iv) meat, (v) cleaning materials, (vi) milk, (vii) wages?

4. A caterer set out to achieve a net profit of 12% on sales. For a wedding reception with 100 guests he estimated the costs as:

Food and drink	£80.00
Labour	£51.00
Overheads	£45.00

a Calculate the total price that should be quoted for the reception if the standard rate of VAT is 8%.
b How much net profit in pounds sterling would the caterer receive?
c After the reception the takings at a private bar were £75 (exclusive of VAT). The average gross profit on the drinks was 55% on sales. Find the gross profit received from the bar.

5. a What is meant by the term 'elements of cost'? In your answer give as much information as you can about each cost with particular reference to the catering industry.

b Under which element of cost should each of the following be placed:

(i) meat, (ii) advertising, (iii) staff accommodation, (iv) staff meals, (v) gas and electricity?

6. a During a certain accounting period a catering manager found that the meat cost was 25% of sales. In the next accounting period the meat cost increased to 30% of sales.
Detail the checks that he could make to try to find the cause of this increase.

b What factors are important in the operation of a successful system of portion control?

7. a The directors of the Makewell Factory agreed to the payment of a direct cash grant of £75 per week towards the food and labour costs of the works canteen. An average of 200 meals are sold on each of the five days per week.
Costs are as follows:

Food cost per meal	£0.25
Total labour cost per week	£125.00

Assuming that no profit or loss is made, calculate the charge per meal (exclusive of VAT).

b Explain the term 'subsidy' with particular reference to works canteens.

c What is the value of the subsidy for each meal in the Makewell Factory canteen?

8. a Out of a delivery of 26 kg of meat it was found that 10 kg were wasted in preparation and cooking. Find the percentage of the delivery that was served.

b (i) A joint of meat takes 2 hours 25 minutes to cook. At what time must the joint be placed in the oven in order order to be cooked at 7.20 p.m.?
(ii) A joint of meat takes 1 hour 55 minutes to cook. At what time (using the 24-hour clock) must the joint be placed in the oven in order to be cooked at 19.45 hrs?

c (i) If 250 g costs 25p, find the cost of 5.25 kg.
(ii) Express 3 kg 40 g in kilograms.

d (i) If the cost of concentrate was 30p per litre, find the cost of 50 ml.
(ii) If 50 ml of concentrate must be added to 250 ml of water, find the cost of concentrate that must be added to 2 litres of water.

EAST MIDLANDS EDUCATIONAL UNION EXAMINATION 1976 FOOD COSTING I

ATTEMPT FIVE QUESTIONS—TIME ALLOWED 1½ HOURS

1. The following figures for the month of February were extracted from the books of the Hill Top Restaurant:

	£
Food cost	800
Full-time labour costs	540
Part-time labour costs	100
Rates	210
Gas and electricity	175
Repairs and renewals	48
Advertising	35
Telephone	25
Stationery	15
Sales	2400

Find as a percentage of sales:

a the gross profit,
b the net profit,
c the labour cost,
d the total costs.

2. Out of a delivery of 75 kg of meat, 35% was wasted in preparation and cooking. The remaining meat was served.

a How many kilograms were served?
b If the portion size was 125 g, how many portions were served?
c The invoice from the butcher showed the total cost of the meat as £108.75. What was the cost per kilogram of the meat bought?

d What factors must be taken into account when deciding on the size of portion to be served?

3. a The food cost of an average school meal was 12.2p.
   (i) If 350 meals were produced on each school day, find the total food cost for one year (assume 1 school week = 5 days and 1 school year = 40 weeks).
   (ii) If the subsidy required for these meals amounted to £10 500 per year, find the subsidy per meal.

b (i) The charge for a restaurant meal was £3.25 + VAT. If the rate of VAT was 8%, calculate the final price for the meal.
   (ii) If the food cost for the meal was £1.05 calculate the gross profit as a percentage of the selling price before the addition of VAT.

c If 2.2 lb = 1 kg, by how much a pound is '15p per pound' cheaper than '38½p per kilogram'?

4. a (i) What is the object of food costing?
   (ii) Give four advantages of food costing.

b What is:
   (i) cash discount,
   (ii) trade discount?

5. Ignore the effect of VAT in this question. Restaurants X and Y have the same food costs and sell the same dishes. Restaurant X worked on a gross profit of 60% of sales. Restaurant Y always watched the prices charged by X and on average charged less.

a X reckoned the food cost of a dish to be 15p.
   (i) What would X charge for this dish?
   (ii) If Y charged 34½p for this dish, find the gross profit received by Y and give your answer as a percentage of the selling price (to the nearest whole figure).

b X charged 80p for a particular dish and sold 100. Y charged 75p and sold 125 of the same dish.
   (i) Find the total gross profit from this dish for X.
   (ii) Find the total gross profit from this dish for Y.

c Give one advantage and one disadvantage in adopting the tactics of Y.

6. Write brief notes to show the meaning and importance of:
a skilled buying,
b careful preparation and cooking,
c portion control,
d correct selling price.

7. a The basic wage rate for a cook was 72p per hour for the first 40 hours worked and 80p per hour for any hours worked in excess of 40 hours.

(i) Calculate the gross wage earned in a week when the cook worked the following hours:

Monday	8.30 a.m.–6.00 p.m
Tuesday	8.30 a.m.–3.30 p.m.
Wednesday	7.30 a.m.–5.00 p.m.
Thursday	7.30 a.m.–5.00 p.m.
Friday	9.00 a.m.–3.45 p.m.
Saturday	8.30 a.m.–5.00 p.m.

All breaks are paid as though worked.

(ii) Write down the times the cook finished on Monday, Tuesday, Wednesday and Friday, using the 24-hour clock.

b A caterer purchased milk at 50p per gallon (only whole gallons were purchased).
Calculate the total profit in a week when 102 one-third pint glasses of milk were sold at 5p each (ignore VAT). Assume any milk not sold in this way is wasted and that the caterer's estimation of requirements is always correct to the whole gallon.

c The takings in a restaurant one day amounted to £270. Find the amount that should be set aside for VAT if the rate of VAT is 8%.

8. a A caterer was in the habit of buying cooking oil from his local supplier in 5 litre containers at £1.85 each. A 'Cash and Carry' store opened five miles away and advertised the cooking oil in 20 litre containers at £6.40 each less a discount of 5% on orders worth £20 or more.

(i) If the caterer uses 15 litres of oil per week calculate how much money would be saved over a 16 week period if the caterer changed to the 'Cash and Carry'.

(ii) What other factor might be considered in addition to the price difference?

b Design a 'bin card' and enter the following details:
Article—Jam

March 1	Balance 20 lb	
March 4	Received 10 lb	Issued 2 lb
March 6	Issued 4 lb	

Note: the minimum stock to be carried is 10 lb.

Answers to exercises

Addition

1. 1344
2. 2182
3. 12 009
3. 10 499
5. 10 038
6. 11 172
7. 9111
8. 9347
9. 60.55
10. 132.09
11. 518.95
12. 760.87
13. 64.32
14. 898.94
15. 803.74
16. 1233.43
17. £144.49
18. £573.86
19. £189.92½
20. £459.62
21. 46.37 kg
22. 230.62 kg
23. 246.04 litres
24. 45.09 litres
25. 49.91
26. 99.71
27. 477.58
28. £65.11
29. £987.84
30. £23.29
31. £2.42
32. £53.40
33. £394.68½
34. £2160.40
35. 7.425 kg
36. 18.35 kg
37. 125.025 kg
38. 68.005 kg
39. 6.175 litres
40. 25.34 litres
41. 130.042 litres
42. 7.006 litres
43. £16.415
44. £22.023
45. £36.338
46. £728.119
47. 169.353 kg
48. 69.047 kg
49. 117.553 litres
50. 157.598 litres

Subtraction

1. 356
2. 1138
3. 3328
4. 5505
5. £14.58
6. £16.78
7. £291.79
8. £464.82
9. 4.95 kg
10. 16.828 kg
11. 7.77 kg
12. 54.975 kg
13. 5.924 litres
14. 75.824 litres
15. 31.979 litres
16. 16.678 litres
17. £12.15
18. £35.72
19. £40.90
20. £9.31½
21. £7.516
22. £0.522
23. 4.5 kg
24. 45.075 kg
25. 4.74 kg
26. 7.198 kg
27. 71.8 litres
28. 10.5 litres
29. 3.875 litres
30. 76.9 litres
31. £361.30
32. 2.484 kg
33. £28.68
34. 21.375 litres

Multiplication

1. 18
2. 40
3. 28
4. 30
5. 72
6. 132
7. 32
8. 84.
9. 27
10. 48
11. 81
12. 48
13. 121
14. 42
15. 36
16. 20
17. 64
18. 60
19. 36
20. 144
21. 870
22. 2569
23. 3264
24. 4000
25. 32 994
26. 72 182
27. 103.8
28. 338.48
29. 74.82
30. £50.58
31. £72.45
32. £126.80
33. £4940.46
34. £4007.64
35. £75.70
36. £34.20
37. £183.664
38. £1053.132
39. £5.02
40. £93.19½
41. £33.86½
42. 31.375 kg
43. 17.712 kg
44. 206.25 kg
45. 2767.5 kg
46. 603.96 kg
47. 4039 kg
48. 121.5 litres
49. 55.65 litres
50. 156.25 litres
51. £43.20
52. £1465.00
53. £140.00
54. 56.4 kg
55. 2105 litres
56. 16 125 kg

Division

1. 8 | **2.** 12 | **3.** 5 | **4.** 8
5. 6 | **6.** 8 | **7.** 10 | **8.** 9
9. 6 | **10.** 9 | **11.** 7 | **12.** 9
13. 11 | **14.** 7 | **15.** 3 | **16.** 7
17. 6 | **18.** 9 | **19.** 5 | **20.** 7
21. 206 | **22.** 509 | **23.** 146 | **24.** 459
25. 504 | **26.** 65 | **27.** 4205 | **28.** 731
29. 265 | **30.** 809 | **31.** 109 | **32.** 2901
33. 17 | **34.** 185 | **35.** 73 | **36.** 4.15
37. 2.81 | **38.** 20.5 | **39.** 123 | **40.** 32
41. 1.5 | **42.** 12.62 | **43.** 1.3475 | **44.** 4.45
45. 2.14 | **46.** 0.452 | **47.** 1.485 | **48.** 4.3
49. 12.9 | **50.** 17.7 | **51.** 9.242 | **52.** 0.655
53. 1.775 | **54.** £2.54 | **55.** 4.642 kg | **56.** £2.49
57. £12.825 | **58.** 2.623 litres | **59.** £21.85 | **60.** 6.24
61. £1.638 | **62.** 4.375 kg | **63.** 14.3 | **64.** 1.827
65. 18.497 | **66.** £49.13 | **67.** 22 kg | **68.** 17.94
69. 3.33 | **70.** £6.467 | **71.** 1.432 | **72.** £0.3642
73. £112.36 | **74.** 4.5 kg | **75.** 4.103 litres | **76.** 0.525 litres

Problems (4 rules)

1. Butter £9, Sugar £2.40, Flour £0.575, Ginger £0.31, Vinegar £0.63, *Total* £12.915
2. $9\frac{1}{2}$p **3. a** £0.76 **b** £0.77 **4.** £26.50 **5. a** £45 **b** £0.15 **6.** 15 **7.** 200

Cancelling

1. $\frac{8}{9}$ | **2.** $\frac{1}{2}$ | **3.** $\frac{7}{9}$ | **4.** $\frac{3}{4}$ | **5.** $\frac{7}{12}$
6. $\frac{1}{3}$ | **7.** $\frac{4}{5}$ | **8.** $\frac{1}{4}$ | **9.** $\frac{3}{4}$ | **10.** $\frac{1}{4}$
11. $\frac{1}{3}$ | **12.** $\frac{4}{5}$

Mixed numbers and improper fractions

1. $\frac{9}{2}$ | **2.** $\frac{12}{5}$ | **3.** $\frac{29}{4}$ | **4.** $\frac{35}{6}$ | **5.** $\frac{32}{3}$
6. $\frac{29}{15}$ | **7.** $\frac{15}{4}$ | **8.** $\frac{16}{7}$ | **9.** $\frac{35}{8}$ | **10.** $\frac{203}{10}$
11. $1\frac{1}{6}$ | **12.** $2\frac{2}{3}$ | **13.** $3\frac{1}{8}$ | **14.** $2\frac{2}{11}$ | **15.** $11\frac{1}{9}$
16. $4\frac{1}{7}$ | **17.** $2\frac{1}{2}$ | **18.** $10\frac{1}{5}$ | **19.** $6\frac{1}{2}$ | **20.** $2\frac{1}{4}$
21. $8\frac{1}{3}$ | **22.** $3\frac{1}{3}$

Multiplication of fractions

1. $\frac{12}{35}$ | **2.** $\frac{25}{48}$ | **3.** $\frac{3}{14}$ | **4.** $\frac{4}{11}$ | **5.** $1\frac{5}{6}$ | **6.** $1\frac{1}{14}$ | **7.** $3\frac{13}{24}$
8. $\frac{7}{10}$ | **9.** 6 | **10.** $6\frac{9}{10}$ | **11.** $2\frac{1}{2}$ | **12.** $5\frac{5}{6}$ | **13.** $13\frac{1}{3}$ | **14.** 26
15. 4 | **16.** $1\frac{3}{10}$ | **17.** $1\frac{3}{8}$ | **18.** $\frac{9}{17}$ | **19.** $9\frac{1}{3}$ | **20.** $5\frac{5}{8}$

Percentages

1. 80% | **2.** 20% | **3.** 47.05% | **4.** 52.5% | **5.** 32%
6. 64.1% | **7.** 45.71% | **8.** 62.5% | **9.** 34.28% | **10.** 45.16%
11. 81.81% | **12.** 66.66% | **13.** 26.66% | **14.** 71.42% | **15.** 17.5%
16. 20.83% | **17.** 40% | **18.** 34.66% | **19.** 66.66% | **20.** 36.03%

Kitchen percentages

1. Soup 3.42%, Meat 25.14%, Vegetables 9.14%, Sweet 9.14%, Tea and Coffee 1.14%.
2. Vegetables 9.6%, Meat 33.6%, Dairy 16%.
3. Meat 59.17%, Vegetables 14.2%, Sweet 17.75%, Drink 8.87%.
4. Dairy 28.73%, Vegetables 13.79%, Meat 57.47%.
5. Milk 5.45%, Tea 11.45%, Sugar 3.63%.
6. Meat 20%, Vegetables 7%, Sweet 5.33%.
7. Meat 20.68%, Vegetables 7.24%, Sweet 5.51%.
8. Increase in meat cost, Increase in wastage, Increase in portion size, Pilfering.

Gross profit

1. 75% **2.** 33.33% **3.** 66.66% **4.** 70% **5.** 37.5%
6. 40% **7.** 53.33% **8.** 50% **9.** 46.15% **10.** 65%
11. 56.25% **12.** 38.57% **13.** 94.44% **14.** 53.33% **15.** 43.75%
16. 60.86% **17.** 54.44% **18.** 5% **19.** 60.6% **20.** 62%

Food cost

1. 35.71% **2. a** 33.33% **b** 66.66% **3.** 30% **4.** 37% **5.** 54.54%

Net profit

1. 10.5% **2. a** 63.58% **b** 9.94% **3.** 10% **4.** £125 **5. a** 40% **b** 90%
6. a £0.60 **b** 13.33% **7.** Net loss 110% **8. a** Yes **b** No **9.** 15.66% **10.** 9.46%
11. a (i) £1100 (ii) 8.8% (iii) £1000 (iv) 10% **b** Discuss **c** A **d** Discuss

More about percentages

1. £5.70 **2.** £14.25 **3.** £3.06 **4.** 4.55 kg
5. 0.25 litres **6.** £1.265 **7.** £13.50 **8.** £62.04
9. £490 **10.** 14 kg **11.** 37.5 litres **12.** 20 kg
13. £1400 **14.** £0.115 **15.** £100 **16.** 14 kg
17. £5000 **18.** £0.555 **19.** 3.75 kg **20.** 32 litres
21. 800 **22.** 18

Percentage problems

1. 440 **2.** £762 **3. a** (i) £0.38 (ii) £5.13 **b** (i) £0.47½ (ii) £5.22½
c (i) £0.57 (ii) £5.32 **4.** 528 **5.** £2750 **6.** £3.82 **7.** £198
8. £840.50 **9.** £25 **10.** £2760 **11.** £698.50 **12.** £624 **13.** 4.4 litres

Discount

1. £36 **2.** B by £13.50 **3.** £340 **4.** £15.30 **5.** Discuss

Percentage puzzles

1. £2 **2.** £13 **3.** 1.5 kg **4.** 5 litres
5. £15.625 **6.** 60 **7.** £0.315 **8.** 60 kg
9. £255 **10.** 20 litres **11.** 90 kg **12.** 120
13. £3.00 **14.** 1 litre **15.** 20

Calculating the selling price

1. £1.80 **2.** £0.50 **3.** £54.55 **4.** £150 **5.** £4.50 **6.** £301
7. a (i) £0.75 (ii) £0.96 (iii) £1.26 **b** Multiply 3 **8.** £4 **9.** £0.70
10. 5p **11.** £0.35 **12.** £5.85 **13.** £4.50 **14.** Discuss **15.** £2.70
16. £156 **17.** £571.42 **18.** 65p **19. a** 63.8% **b** £66.50 **20.** Discuss

Wastage

1. 40% **2.** 70% **3.** 20 kg **4.** 42 kg **5.** 13 kg **6.** 22 kg **7.** £99 **8.** 56 kg

Bin cards

1. 19 kg **2.** 24 × 5 kg **3.** 29 **4.** 14.25 kg **5.** 10 × 250 g **6.** 126

Finding the cost of food and drink used

1. £65 **2.** £250 **3.** £19 550 **4.** £456 **5.** £490
6. £1050 **7.** £665 **8.** £85 **9.** £2208 **10.** £8000
11. **a** (i)£595 (ii) £575 **b** Discuss

Costing sheets

1.

	£
Eggs	0.2
sugar	0.04
flour	0.03
butter	0.062
Total	0.332
portion cost	0.041

2.

	£
flour	0.045
sugar	0.02
margarine	0.065
Total	0.13
portion cost	0.01

3.

	£
flour	0.09
b. powder	0.005
sugar	0.022
suet	0.108
currants	0.108
Total	0.333
portion cost	0.055

4.

	£
milk	0.135
sugar	0.04
butter	0.031
jam	0.03
eggs	0.15
Total	0.386
portion cost	0.096

5.

	£
beef	1.30
sugar	0.006
onion	0.04
beer	0.162
Total	1.508
portion cost	0.377

6.

	£
lamb	0.51
potatoes	0.036
celery	0.022
b. onions	0.045
onions	0.02
leeks	0.048
Total	0.681
portion cost	0.17

Graphs

1. £2000 **2.** June **3.** Christmas and New Year trade **4.** 180
5. Saturday **6.** Wednesday, Thursday **7.** **a** £1700 **b** £1400 **c** £300
8. £300 **9.** Week 5 **10.** Week 9

Pie Charts

1. Wages £5600, Insurance £480, Accommodation £160, Travel £160, Staff meals £800.
2. Food and Drink 144°, Labour 90°, Overheads 72°, Net Profit 54°.
3. Accommodation 240°, Food 80°, Drink and Tobacco 40°.
4. Food £80 000, Labour £35 000, Overheads £45 000, Net Profit £20 000.

Currency conversion

1. £500 **2.** 3750 pesetas **3.** £10.60 **4.** 83 750 lire **5.** 75 000 pesetas
6. £29.25 **7.** 472 dollars **8.** 123.75 francs **9.** 3000 pesetas.

Twenty-four hour clock

1. 05.00 **2.** 12.25 **3.** 22.00 **4.** 02.10 **5.** 11.27 **6.** 12.00 **7.** 23.55 **8.** 15.00 **9.** 3 a.m. **10.** 5.30 p.m. **11.** 12.15 a.m. **12.** 4 p.m. **13.** 10.20 p.m. **14.** 11.28 a.m. **15.** 8.05 p.m. **16.** 1 p.m. **17.** 19.05 **18.** 14.40 **19.** 09.50 **20.** 16.50 **21.** Dish A 18.15, Dish B 17.35, Dish C 19.00, Dish D 18.25 **22.** 00.49 **23.** 00.02

Test 1

1. £996.03 **2.** £667.69 **3.** £16 032.64 **4.** £0.63 **5. a** £120 **b** 26 kg **6.** £14 **7.** £39.30 **8. a** $\frac{2}{3}$ **b** $\frac{1}{6}$ **c** $\frac{3}{20}$ **9. a** $\frac{2}{7}$ **b** $\frac{6}{11}$ **c** $2\frac{1}{2}$ **10.** 15p

Test 2

1. £4.31 **2.** £260 **3.** £132 **4.** £104.90½ **5.** £4.80 **6.** Meat 10.9%, Vegetables 6.9%, Sweets 7.27%, Tea and Coffee 1.27%. **7.** 4.372 kg **8.** £1.125 **9.** £104 **10.** 8.75%.

Test 3

1. a 66.11% **b** 10.55% **2.** 21 kg **3.** £66.80 **4.** £61.25 **5.** £0.97 **6.** 66.66% **7.** £546 **8.** 60% **9.** 15p **10. a** £2000 **b** £2.05

Test 4

1. a £0.18 **b** (i) £0.45 (ii) £0.27 **c** 64% **2. a** £376 **b** 62.4% **3. a** £200.25 **b** £0.44 **4.** £0.65 **5.** £39 **6.** £0.12

Test 5

1. Graph **2. a** Meat 15.4%, Vegetables 9.25%, Dry goods 10.45%, Beverages 3.65% **b** Price rise, Increase in wastage, Portion control poor, pilfering. **3. a** £0.615 **b** £1.125 **4. a** (i) $2\frac{7}{8}$ (ii) $3\frac{1}{17}$ **b** (i) $\frac{23}{7}$ (ii) $\frac{58}{5}$ **5. a** 250 **b** £0.50 **6. a** 66.66% **b** 18.83% **c** 26.66% **d** 81.17%

Test 6

1. £3.90 **2. a** 20 kg **b** 66.66% **3.** £29.80 **4. a** £14.01 **b** £25.18 **c** £0.85 **5.** 94.36% **6. a** 60.96% **b** £0.88 **c** £877.80

Test 7

1. a £0.18 **b** £14.21 **c** £0.87 **2.** 16 kg **3. a** (i) £1566 (ii) £2434 **b** £804 **4. a** £0.48 **b** £1.20 **c** 68% **5. a** 3025 g **b** 7.148 kg **c** 4250 ml **d** 6.035 litres **6. a** Finding best price—cuts costs. Correct quality for dish avoids wastage. Reliable supplier avoids problems of storage. **b** Avoids wastage. Customer satisfaction. **c** Accurate costing. Customer satisfaction. **d** Avoids money loss.

Test 8

1. a Materials (food and drink), Labour, Overheads. **b** (i) Overheads (ii) Labour (iii) Food (iv) Overheads (v) Overheads **2. a** 25 kg **b** £81.25 **3 a** (i) 65% (ii) 60% (iii) 62.85% **b** 54.83% **4. a** 66.66% **b** 18% **c** 25.07% **5. a** £2.70 **b** £2.75 **c** £2.80 **6.** £49.55

Test 9

1. a (i) £925 (ii) £90 (iii) 9.72% **b** Net loss **2.** Increase in price charged by 5% **3. a** (i) £415 (ii) £440 **b** (i) 68.07% (ii) 66.15% **c** Discuss **4. a** £0.35 **b** £0.425 **5.** Graph **6.** Reliability, portion control, cost control, pricing uniformity.

Test 10

1. a £2.375 **b** 8.09% **2. a** (i) £0.94 (ii) £0.12 (iii) 70% **b** Gross profit
3. a 65.6% **b** 13.58% **c** 26.94% **d** 86.42% **4.** 59.14%

Test 11

1. a £778 **b** 56% **2. a** £38.295 **b** 95.73% **c** (i) £32.47 (ii) 96.2% (iii) 8p
Discuss **3. a** 42 kg **b** 38 kg **c** A **d** Discuss **4. a** (i) £250 (ii) £325
b (i) £475 (ii) £725

Test 12

1. a £180 **b** £514 **c** 22.22% **2. a** £0.15 **b** £0.375 **c** 70% **3. a** £1420
b 66.19% **c** 16% **4.** £2.70

Test 13

1. a (i) A 67.18% B 63.15% (ii) A 27.18% B 25.26% (iii) A 28% B 25.89%
(iv) A 12% B 12% **b** A—larger % spent on labour and overheads. Smaller % on food.
2. Food and Drink cost could remain the same % of sales but labour and overheads would not increase in proportion to sales.
3. a £25 **b** 58.33% **4. a** £7230 **b** 62.14% **c** graph

Test 14

1. a £41 **b** Yes, loss is £675 instead of £2400 **c** 95.95% **2. a** £611 **b** 60.06%
c £216 **3.** A £1.93 B £2.75 C £5.50 **4.** Discuss

E.M.E.U. examination 1973

1. a (i) £33.75 (ii) £0.27 **b** £0.208 **c** (i) £10 (ii) 5½p
2. a £47.49 **b** Discussion
3. a 66.66% **b** 18% **c** 23.58% **d** 82%
4. a (i) 50.909 kg (ii) 22.222 litres (iii) £0.09 (iv) ½p **b** 4.35 kg
5. Discussion
6. a (i) £0.625 (ii) £1.60 (iii) £0.075 **b** Discussion, should include; profit required, ability of customers to pay, portion size, competition, turnover, reputation, facilities. **c** VAT increases the price of the meal.
7. a Meat 26.31%, Vegetables 16.05%, Sweets 17.1%.
b (i) 30%, (ii) Discussion
8. a (i) £850 (ii) £825 **b** 1% **c** Manager (ii) No but attitudes are slowly changing on this matter due to the effect of inflation—discussion.

E.M.E.U. examination 1975

1. a (i) £1308 (ii) 86% **b** (i) £0.96 (ii) £2892.50 **c** (i) 2.2 lbs (ii) 1.8 pints.
2. a (i) £30.725 (ii) £25.08 **b** Goods have arrived. Arithmetic is accurate. Date to earn discount. Goods were authorised, etc.
3. a (i) £300 (ii) 62.5% **b** (i) £400 (ii) 66.66% **c** potatoes, meat, milk.
4. a £216 **b** £24 **c** £41.25
5. a Materials (food and drink), labour, overheads.
b (i) Materials (ii) Overheads (iii) Labour (iv) Labour (v) Overheads
6. a Check for wastage (buying, storage, preparation and cooking), portion control, price movement, pilfering, etc. **b** Discussion.
7. a £0.30 **b** Discussion **c** £0.075
8. a 61.53% **b** (i) 4.55 p.m. (ii) 17.50 hrs. **c** (i) £5.25 (ii) 3.040 kg
d (i) £0.015 (ii) 400 ml.

E.M.E.U. examination 1976

1. **a** 66.66% **b** 18.83% **c** 26.66% **d** 81.1%
2. **a** 48.75 kg **b** 390 C £1.45 **d** Discussion. Profit, price type of customer, etc.
3. **a** (i) £8450 (ii) 15p **b** (i) £3.51 (ii) 67.69% **c** 2½p
4. Discussion
5. **a** (i) 37½p (ii) 57% **b** (i) £48 (ii) £53.75 **c** Discussion
6. Discussion
7. **a** (i) £37.40 (ii) Mon. 18.00 Tues, 15.30 Wed 17.00 Fri. 15.45 **b** £0.60 **c** £20
8. **a** (i) £15.84 (ii) Discussion **b** March 6th balance 24 lbs.

Index

lifelong goal and filled him with a sense of purpose. He had spent the previous night in a cell, already bruised from a savage beating at the hands of some soldiers. But this Friday had been planned before time began; it would herald an event that was going to change history and give rise to an act that would affect people's eternity. It was the day that he was going to lay down his life, so that countless people could enter into a relationship with God.

Living for a cause

Both men gave their lives for a cause, but they were motivated by very different beliefs. The first man had tragically been poisoned by a message of vengeance and hatred. The second man, Jesus, was filled with love, and accomplished a mission that brought people life rather than death.

How would Jesus respond to the London bombings?

We are still coming to terms with the terrible events that took place in London. But as we respond to the evil that has taken place, we should be careful not to get drawn into the mindset that drove the perpetrators, and, as a result, be filled with anger and bitterness. The Bible describes Christians as 'ambassadors for Christ' and this means that we should respond to this appalling event in a way that is worthy of the man who laid down his life for the right reasons. So, we need to stand back from the initial impact of these events, see what the Bible says about it, and respond in a way that is modelled on Jesus' life, death and teaching.

The spectre of suffering

When an atrocity like this occurs, the inevitable question people ask is, 'Why?' Although this is natural, it is often asked because we see suffering and tragedy as things that should not happen in our lives and our country. It is an enemy that has breached our defences but should really belong elsewhere. The truth of the matter is that we have a human tendency to cocoon ourselves from the massive volume of suffering that goes on in the world, and pretend that it does not exist. However, the Bible does not keep up such a pretence; when sin first came into the world, God said, 'Cursed is the ground because of you; through painful toil you will eat of it all the days of your life. It will produce thorns and thistles for you, and you will eat the plants of the field. By the sweat of your brow you will eat your food until you

...we see suffering and tragedy as things that should not happen in our lives and our country.

return to the ground, since from it you were taken; for dust you are and to dust you will return' (Genesis 3:17-19). Paradise was lost, life grew hard, and suffering became embedded into our existence. Near the end of his life, Moses wrote a psalm which echoed this theme. He said: 'All our days pass away under your wrath; we finish our years with a moan. The length of our days is seventy years—or eighty, if we have the strength; yet their span is but trouble and sorrow, for they quickly pass, and we fly away' (Psalm 90:9-10). And Job, a man who knew intense suffering in his life, said, 'Affliction does not come from the dust, Nor does trouble spring from the ground; Yet man is born to trouble, As the sparks fly upward' (Job 5:6-7, NKJV).

The theme continues in the New Testament. Jesus was born into a nation that had been occupied by one of the most ruthless powers in history—the Roman Empire. Luke's Gospel tells us that the events surrounding Jesus' birth took place in the days when Herod ruled the province of Judea (Luke 1:5) and these were days of untold tyranny and oppression. Jesus was executed in one of the most brutal ways imaginable. In fact, a Jewish historian described crucifixion as 'the most terrible and cruel death which man has ever devised to take vengeance on his fellow man.'[2] All but one of the apostles died for their faith, and thousands of early Christians were put to the sword, thrown to the lions, covered in pitch and set on fire. The Bible never pretends that suffering, tragedy and disaster do not exist. Rather, it reminds us that they have been in the world since sin came into existence.

In the months leading up to the violent events in London, there have been suicide bombings in Iraq and Israel, conflict and famine in Africa, and a tsunami in Asia. The world is riddled with suffering, but we, in the United Kingdom, have been relatively cushioned from it. Suffering is the result of humanity's separation from God. It is inevitable since the Fall and will continue until Jesus returns.

Is this God's judgement?

When Jesus was told about an atrocity, Pilate, the Roman Governor of Judea had committed against the Galileans, he said: 'Do you think that these Galileans were worse sinners than all the other Galileans because they suffered this way? I tell you, no! But unless you repent, you too will all perish. Or those eighteen who died when the tower in Siloam fell on them—do you think they were more guilty than all the others living in Jerusalem? I tell you, no! But unless

you repent, you too will all perish' (Luke 13:2-5). No one has the authority to say that such terrible events are specific judgements from God. However, because the human race has chosen to ignore God and live in rebellion against him, he does not necessarilly intervene to prevent such outrages. Jesus' words remind us that such things point us to our need to get right with God. The final judgement, which God will bring about, will be far worse and more devastating than any contemporary event. That judgement is delayed to give people the opportunity to find forgiveness through his Son.

The final judgement, which God will bring about, will be far worse and more devastating than any contemporary event.

Life is fragile

For most people travelling into London, July 7th was just another working day. Thousands of people crowded on to railway platforms in towns and suburbs around the city, buried their heads in their newspapers, and prepared themselves for another day at the office or in the shop. For many of them, death would have been the last thing on their minds. But, for some, it came swiftly and unexpectedly. This is a reminder that we do not know when death may whisk us away from this world. James, a writer in the New Testament, talks about this, saying, 'Now listen, you who say, "Today or tomorrow we will go to this or that city, spend a year there, carry on business and make money." Why, you do not even know what will happen tomorrow. What is your life? You are a mist that appears for a little while and then vanishes' (James 4:13-17). This makes me think how quickly steam vanishes almost the instant a window is opened. People may achieve great things in their life and hold impressive positions but, like the millions of people who were on the earth before them, they will live for a short time and then die. An event like this is an important reminder that life, for everyone, is brief and may come to an end unexpectedly. We need to make sure that we are right with God and encourage others to be right with him, too. There isn't a moment to lose!

An event like this is an important reminder that life, for everyone, is brief and may come to an end unexpectedly.

Forgiveness and Justice

After the initial shock, most of us will feel very angry about the horrifying events that have taken

place in our capital city. While it is wrong to be bitter and vengeful towards the people responsible, the Bible does say, 'Be angry and do not sin' (Ephesians 4:26, ESV). We have a right to be angry with people who fill young people's minds with hatred, and feed them with the lie that if they strap bombs to themselves and ignite them in a crowded area, they will be given a fast track to paradise. But, although we should be angry at the masterminds of the atrocity and the bombers themselves, the anger the Bible speaks of is more significant. It involves our standing back and seeing this act within the context of the whole of the sinful reality that exists in our fallen world. This is not personal vengeance and it will never poison us against a particular segment of our society. In the New Testament, we are commanded not to take revenge but rather to leave this with God. 'For it is written: "It is mine to avenge; I will repay," says the Lord' (Romans 12:19). Instead, we should channel our anger into a

> ...on a personal level, Jesus also calls his disciples to display an attitude of forgiveness.

desire for justice, which God has given us for situations such as this. The men who unleashed the carnage on London on 7/7 may have believed that they were on a path to paradise, but they will find themselves standing before 'the judge of all the earth' who will call them to account for their wicked acts.

The New Testament teaches that although final justice will be brought about by God, in this world it should be carried out by the state. In the book of Romans, the person who governs us is described as 'God's servant, an agent of wrath to bring punishment on the wrongdoer' (Romans 13:4). So we should support and pray for the authorities in their efforts to bring to justice those who planned the attack. On a personal level, Jesus also calls his disciples to display an attitude of forgiveness, in the knowledge that God himself will ultimately bring true judgement and justice to every evil act. Only this will break the cycle of hate and prejudice that fuels these kinds of atrocities.

In the wake of a fatal shooting in a school in the USA (which also involved the suicide of the murderers), people left flowers to express their shock and sorrow at what had happened. Someone hung a sign above them saying, 'These flowers and prayers are for the innocent victims and their families, not for the monsters who committed this selfish act.' After seeing the way this intensified the mood of hatred, a woman laid down a bouquet of flowers and said, 'I want to give them to the monsters too.' She was not excusing or justifying their wicked act, but she did want to show that there could be a different response to hatred and bitterness, which would stop the poison going deeper. She was following a principle set out in the Bible: 'Do not be overcome by evil, but overcome evil with good' (Romans 12:21, NKJV).

Can we draw comfort from judgement?

The terrible events in London are part of a bigger cycle of violence, disaster, suffering and death that is taking place around the world. Jesus said that these things would happen increasingly as his return draws nearer. 'You will hear of wars and rumours of wars, but see to it that you are not alarmed. Such things must happen, but the end is still to come. Nation will rise against nation, and kingdom against kingdom. There will be famines and earthquakes in various places. All these are the beginning of birth-pains' (Matthew 24:6-8). At the moment, we are outraged at the way in which people have been indiscriminately massacred by suicide bombers in London, Iraq, Turkey and Israel. But we can draw comfort from the fact that Jesus will

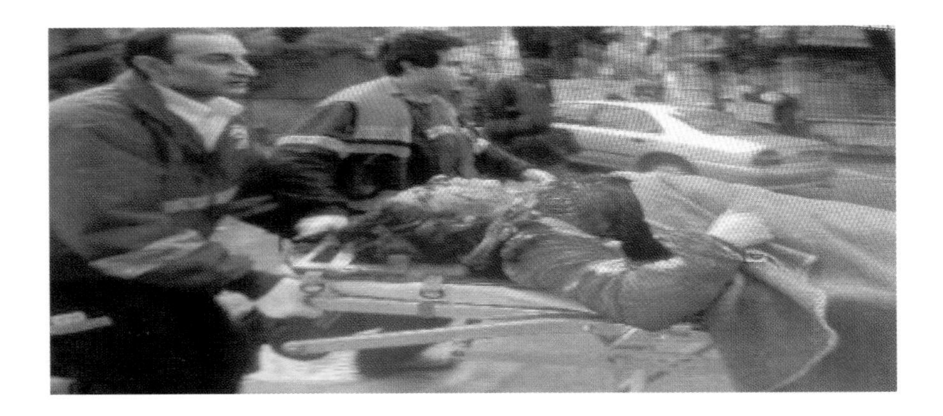

return as judge (Acts 10:42). A lot of people do not like the idea of a Day of Judgement, but if they were to think about it in the light of these terrible events, they would realize that it is a good thing. In fact, it would be terrible if there were no final judgement, because the people behind the atrocities in London and around the world would get away with the evil acts they have committed. Without a Day of Judgement, there would be no ultimate justice.

If I were to stop and talk to people in London and ask them if they thought it was a good thing that the people who planned and executed these acts of terrorism will be brought to justice by God, most would say 'yes'. But, the reality is that although we may not be responsible for such terrible acts, every one of us has done something wrong for which we will answer to the Judge. The New Testament says that 'all have sinned and fall short of the glory of God' (Romans 3:23, NKJV). Sin is rebellion against God. It involves people rejecting him and choosing to do as they like, rather than obeying his commands.

If we want other people to be brought to God's justice, we must be prepared to face it ourselves. But

The New Testament says that 'all have sinned and fall short of the glory of God' (Romans 3:23)

how can we be sure of what will happen to us? After telling people that God had appointed Jesus as the final Judge, Peter said, 'All the prophets testify about him that everyone who believes in him receives forgiveness of sins through his name' (Acts 10:43). Having experienced unspeakable violence and endured excruciating pain on the cross, Jesus said to his Father, 'My God, my God, why have you forsaken me?' (Mark 15:34). He was not questioning why this was happening; he was talking about the fact that he had been separated from God. When Jesus went to the cross, he took our place, he faced God's justice, and he received the punishment for our sins. He was separated from God so that we need never be. We receive forgiveness by facing up to the fact that we have rebelled, by turning to God, realizing that Jesus has paid the penalty for our sin, and by trusting him alone.

On April 20th 1999, two disaffected young men walked into their high school in Columbine, Colorado, USA, and killed twenty-two of their fellow-pupils and a teacher, before turning their guns on themselves. This dreadful event devastated the people in the community and traumatized the

young people who survived. But a group of Christians from the school met to grieve and pray together, asking God what they could do in response. They decided to use a church building near to the school and make themselves available to young people who were distressed. There was a huge response, and these young Christians spent time listening to them, crying with them and bringing comfort to them. When the minister of the church was asked why he thought it was so effective, he said, 'Some wanted to make sense of the deaths. I don't think we can. Others would say, "Where can I turn? Is there any hope? Is there any comfort?" That's the issue we addressed loud and clear.'

There are two ways to respond to the atrocities that have taken place in London. There is the way of hatred, fear and vengeance. This is no different from the mindset that motivated the people who were behind the bombings. Or there is the way that Jesus took, and which he calls us to follow: repentance, faith, the way of forgiveness, love, and trust in God, who has appointed his Son to be the Judge.

Some points from the Bible to think about...

God...now commands all people everywhere to repent. For he has set a day when he will judge the world with justice by the man he has appointed. He has given proof of this to all men by raising him from the dead. (Acts 17:30, 31)

Jesus answered, 'I am the way and the truth and the life. No one comes to the Father except through me.' (John 14:6)

Seek the LORD while he may be found; call upon him while he is near. Let the wicked forsake his way and the evil man his thoughts. Let him turn to the LORD, and he will have mercy on him, and to our God, for he will freely pardon. (Isaiah 55:6, 7).

To this you were called, because Christ suffered for you, leaving you an example, that you should follow in his steps. 'He committed no sin, and no deceit was found in his mouth.' When they hurled their insults at him, he did not retaliate; when he suffered, he made no threats. Instead, he entrusted himself to him who judges justly. He himself bore our sins in his body on the tree, so that we might die to sins and live for righteousness; by his wounds you have been healed. (1 Peter 2:21-24)

'I am the way and the truth and the life. No one comes to the Father except through me.' (John 14:6)

NOTES

1 This detail was given by Ben Macintyre in Times newspaper, 16 July 2005

2 Quoted by David Watson, in 'Discipleship', Hodder and Stoughton, London, 1981, page 237

The author: Simon J Robinson is minister of the Walton Evangelical Church, Chesterfield, England, and author of several books published by Day One.

Scripture quotations are from The New International Version, unless otherwise noted.

British Library Cataloguing in Publication Data available.

If you require further copies of this booklet, please contact us for details

Day One Publications
Ryelands Road
Leominster HR6 8NZ
sales@dayone.co.uk
www.dayone.co.uk
☎ 01568 613 740
FAX 01568 611 473

In the United States
Day One Publications
PO Box 1047
129 Mobilization Drive Waynesboro
GA 30830-2047
☎ Toll Free 1-8 More Books

In Canada

Day One Publications
Sola Scriptura
350 Speedvale Avenue West
Unit 11
Guelph
Ontario, N1H 7M7
☎ 519 763 0339

No part of this publication may be reproduced, or stored in a retrieval system, or transmitted, in any form or by any means, mechanical, electronic, photocopying, recording or otherwise, without the prior permission of Day One Publications.

© **Day One** 2005
All rights reserved